THE SECRET OF THE SAINTS

THE SECRET OF THE SAINTS

STUDIES IN PRAYER, MEDITATION AND SELF-DISCIPLINE

BY

SIR HENRY S. LUNN
M.A., M.D., B.Ch. Trin. Coll., Dublin

Τῇ ἐκκλησίᾳ τοῦ Θεοῦ, κλητοῖς ἁγίοις.
Πάντα γὰρ ὑμῶν ἐστιν.

CAMBRIDGE
W. HEFFER & SONS LTD
1933

LONDON AGENTS
SIMPKIN MARSHALL LTD.

PRINTED IN ENGLAND

THESE PAGES ARE DEDICATED

TO THE MEMORY OF

MY FRIEND AND LEADER

DR. CHARLES HENRY BRENT

BISHOP OF WESTERN NEW YORK

AND PRESIDENT OF

THE WORLD CONFERENCE OF FAITH AND ORDER

HELD AT LAUSANNE IN AUGUST, 1927

Preface

THE Wesleyan Methodist Conference of 1930 appointed a Committee on Corporate Prayer, of which I am a member. In considering how I could best serve the purpose for which that Committee came into being and help in the work which it is hoping to do, it seemed possible that I might prepare a useful volume on the teaching of the saints in all ages upon the duty of prayer, meditation and discipline. I was encouraged thereto by the fact that more leisure would be mine, as I was just ending my editorship of *The Review of the Churches*, begun forty years earlier. An incident that happened at the farewell dinner which my Editorial Council gave me in October, 1930, was a further inspiration for this task. The Archbishop of Canterbury, who presided on that occasion, said in the course of his speech, that a little book of prayers which I had published twenty years earlier called "The Love of Jesus" had been his constant companion. Mr. Walter Runciman also said that he carried this little manual with him on his journeys. I was, therefore, emboldened to hope that the reading of a long life and my editorial experiences, and the new leisure that came with the resignation of my editorship, might help me to produce a volume which would aid the readers in the first and greatest of all duties of the spiritual life.

In this work I have been greatly encouraged by the counsel of some of those associated with me as members of the Editorial Committee of *The Review of the Churches*, and other intimate friends of many communions, who have read the proofs and have given their unofficial imprimatur to these pages. Their names are:—

Anglican.—The late Bishop of Winchester, the Bishop of Leicester, the Bishop of Plymouth, the Dean of Chichester, the Dean of Winchester, Archdeacon Rawlinson, Canon Mozley, the Rev. Prebendary Mackay, and the Rev. Arnold Pinchard.

Baptist.—The Rev. Charles Brown, the Rev. Thomas Phillips, and C. T. Le Quesne, K.C.

Congregationalist.—The Rev. Albert Peel, the Rev. Principal Selbie, and the Rev. E. Shillito.

Methodist.—The Rev. Walter Armstrong, the Rev. Benjamin Gregory, the Rev. A. W. Harrison, Edmund S. Lamplough, the Rev. Frederic Platt, J. Arthur Rank, the Rev. J. E. Rattenbury, the Rev. J. Scott Lidgett, the Rev. F. L. Wiseman, and the Rev. H. B. Workman.

Presbyterian.—The Rev. G. S. Duncan, David
    Russell, LL.D., the Rev. P. Carnegie
    Simpson and the Rev. Hubert Simpson.

A personal note must be added in presenting this
little book to the reader. My life is now drawing
nearer to its close. More than threescore and ten
years are passed, and as the final goal of this
pilgrimage approaches, it is well to place on record
the lessons that a long life has taught of the way
of access to the throne of the Divine Mercy. And
though that record reveals a gulf between the
lessons and the life, one is comforted by the
words of the author of *The Cloud of Unknowing*,
"Not what thou art, nor what thou hast been,
seeth the Lord with His merciful eyes, but what
thou wouldest be."

The Meditations on pages 165—192 reveal the
spirit of helplessness and dependence upon God in
which this book has been written. At no time
have the burdens of life been heavier than in the
months which have passed since this work began.
Nevertheless, in the valley of humiliation, it has
been possible to say, "I will fear no evil, for Thou
art with me." And now my hope is that in the
years to come some may be helped by the experiences which have made these pages possible. In
such experiences God teaches lessons of communion with Him and submission to His will.

I have endeavoured to write this book in the spirit of the words of William Law: "If we would be true Christians of the Catholic Church, we must enter into a Catholic affection for all men, love the spirit of the Gospel wherever we see it, not work ourselves up into an abhorrence of a George Fox, or an Ignatius Loyola, but be equally glad of the light of the Gospel, wherever it shines or from whatever quarter it comes." With Stephen Hobhouse in his preface to his book on William Law I would also say: "I pray that nothing written in this book may encourage the critical spirit at the expense of the spirit of prayer and of love, on the increase of which William Law's great heart was set."

I should like to express my gratitude to all who, by counsel and in other ways, have assisted me in the preparation of these pages.

My obligation to many writers is expressed in the bibliography contained in the closing pages of this book. By the kind permission of the Rev. Gilbert Shaw I have printed his valuable and helpful "Pilgrim's Chapbook" as an Appendix.

HENRY S. LUNN.

Hastings,
Ash Wednesday, 1933.

Redeemer from sin, but also assert that no
deemer is needed, that sin is not sin, and that
rals should be based, not on self-denial and self-
trol, but on the full expression of self. The
edy through which the Russian Church and
on are passing is but an extreme illustration
moral anarchy which exists to a greater or
degree in all lands, and which threatens the
ity of society as our fathers have known it.
sia has experienced a more severe and more
read persecution than any that the Church
Universal has ever known even in the
look darkest days of Diocletian's reign, or
that of the Sultan Abdul Ahmed. We
confess, perhaps because in 1914–18
became commonplace, that we have
ved by too little sympathy with the
m of thousands of bishops and clergy
reds of thousands of their people. Even
n death has been the forced atheistic
f children and youths, who have been
o blaspheme the name of our Lord, and
underfoot all the moral laws of Go
hich have raised our race above th
brutes.
ve say, "Westward look, the land i
cross the Atlantic our friends an
onfronted with the gravest problems
t by their remarkable success i

Contents

The Secret of the

THE NEED OF AN APOSTOL

THE supreme need of the wh
in all lands to-day is an
The dust of conflict and th
scarcely passed away fr
still watches nation acros
armed, and guarded by r
War. Notwithstanding
people can say whole-he
burden of costly arma
ensue it." We as c
endeavours made t
creasingly bitter w
universal breaking
always marks the
its legacy in a
itself in the writ
men not only de
but also for the
dom assail th
the Mount.

a
Re
mo
con
trag
Nat
of a
less
stabil
Rus
widesp

The Out
East and
West

horrors
been mo
martyrdo
and hund
worse tha
teaching o
compelled
to trample
and man w
level of the
Nor can
bright." A
kinsmen are
brought abou

material things. It is not merely that extreme crime is rampant, but the demoralisation of corruption has seriously affected the life of the Churches, and notable scandals among those holding high office in Church and State give cause for much misgiving as to the future of Christianity on that Continent, and for grave fear lest it fail in the endeavour to overcome the evils of materialism.

We have been compelled by these facts to ask ourselves whether, in the lives of our own nation and the other nations of western Europe, the amazing and constantly increasing victories of science, by which man has wrested new power and new riches from nature, have not also led us and our fellows to rest too much in the enjoyment of the things seen and temporal, and dimmed our vision of, and weakened our faith in, the eternal realities, the hold upon which enabled our fore-fathers to "spread scriptural holiness" through this and other lands. We rejoice in everything that truly enriches the lives of the poor, and brings within reach of the unprivileged, opportuni-ties of physical and intellectual culture. At the same time, we know in our inmost hearts the danger of dwelling upon these temporal possessions, and saying, "We are rich and increased in goods, and have need of nothing," when really we have failed to lay up treasure in heaven, and have

missed opportunities of real enrichment in the
eternal treasures. Therefore, we must begin our
prayers with true penitence, and confession of
sins, of the weakness of our love of God, and the
inevitable consequent feebleness of our service for
man. In order that our approach to the footstool
of the Divine Compassion may be marked by a
deep consciousness of our own failures, we must
take to ourselves the warnings and rebukes in
the message of the exile of Patmos to the seven
Churches of Asia. That they were needful within
the lifetime of those who had witnessed our Lord's
Passion and Death, and had shared in His promised
gift of the Holy Spirit for the early Church, leaves
us no room to hope that such warnings are not
necessary for us.

In our own country we do well to take the
testimony of those whose position gives them
authority to speak. A recent writer
**The
weakening
of the habit
of Prayer**
has told us that when an English
diocesan Bishop lately issued a questionnaire to all his clergy as to their
teaching and practice of prayer, he did
not receive a single answer. A well-known
conductor of retreats, Father Conran of the Society
of St. John the Evangelist, Cowley, stated recently
in the *Church Times* that "it is generally recognised
that our people to-day hardly pray at all." A
questionnaire similarly issued to superintendent

Ministers of Wesleyan Methodism for the information of the Committee on Corporate Prayer, has brought a response that is no more encouraging than the silence which greeted the Bishop's enquiry.

The following are some of the replies to the Methodist questionnaire:—"Prayer," says one "is more a problem than a practice." Another writes: "The majority of Methodists have no interest in prayer." Yet another says: "I have come to the conclusion that Methodism, as I know it, has lost the desire for social prayer, and unlike Mr. B——, I am both hopeless and helpless."

Whether we contrast our lives with the record contained in the letters of Samuel Rutherford in the seventeenth century; or with the men of the "Holy Club" at Oxford at the beginning of the eighteenth century, with their rigorous discipline and "tremendous strivings after God and goodness;" or with the days of fasting and prayer which marked the lives of men like John Fletcher, Vicar of Madeley, the greatest saint of the Evangelical revival, who made it his rule to sit up two whole nights every week for reading, meditation and prayer; or with the prayer habits of William Wilberforce and the "Clapham Sect"; the children of the Evangelical Revival at the end of the eighteenth century; or with the Founders of the Oxford Movement—Pusey, Keble, and their fellows, summoning a nation to prayer by their example and teaching; in every case the conclusion is inevitable, that *their apostolate was an apostolate of prayer*. In many things they differed widely from each other; Benedict and Wilberforce, Bernard of Clairvaux, and William Penn of Philadelphia, each faced his own widely differing problems and necessities. Nevertheless, it is in "the secret place of the Most High" that each of these men and every Apostle has been equipped for service from Pentecost until to-day.

Whilst we bow in penitence before the Love that emptied Himself of all for us men and for our

Pentecost

salvation, we find encouragement in the history of the Church to believe that persistent prayer is the divinely chosen method for equipping the soldiers of the Cross with all that is needful to enable them to prevail against the gates of Hell. Again and again, all down the centuries this has been proved to be true. The travail which preceded Pentecost is thus described by St. Luke, "These all continued with one accord in prayer and supplication with the women."—"All with one accord." The gift of tongues of fire was not confined to the chosen twelve, but in that upper room, about 120—men and women—were fitted for the greatest duty that mortals have ever known, to be witnesses unto the Christ, "unto the uttermost parts of

the earth." For this equipment they had spent
those ten days after the Ascension in corporate
prayer, and then the promise of their Lord had
been fulfilled, and the Church of 3,000 of those
who were being saved was born in a day.

We know that these men and women of Pentecost inherited a great legacy in the corporate

Prayer in the Jewish Church prayer of the Jewish Church. At
sundry times and in divers manners the
prophets from Moses onwards had
spoken to God in the name of, and in
the presence of, all the people.

"Lord, Thou hast been our dwelling place in all
generations" are the opening words of that
majestic anthem—the psalm of Moses—which
countless millions in all ages have used in common
worship—"A thousand years in Thy sight are but
as yesterday when it is past. We spend our years
as a tale that is told. So teach us to number our
days that we may get us a heart of wisdom."
Thus in united prayer, adoration, and petition,
have succeeding generations joined in the one
body in which the faithful of all ages approach
God the Transcendent, the Infinite, the Majestic.

"We who have not seen Thy Face,
    By faith, and faith alone, embrace"

—and that faith is strengthened and confirmed from
age to age by the prayer and praise of the whole
Jewish Church.

"Will God in very deed dwell upon earth? Behold Heaven and the Heaven of Heavens cannot contain Thee, how much less this house which I have built," are the words of Solomon as in the presence of the assembled nation he opens up the way for the finite to approach the Infinite. "If Thy People sin against Thee (for there is no man that sinneth not) and Thou be angry with them, and deliver them over before their enemies, and they bethink themselves and turn and say 'We have sinned!' then hear Thou from the heavens, Thy dwelling place, and forgive." The thousands who joined in this great petition at that dedicatory service are but as a grain of sand out of the limitless shores of the ocean, in comparison with the innumerable multitude who have found in those sentences hope to encourage them when overcome by temptation and sin, and assure them that the Infinite and the Eternal looks down from Heaven upon the gatherings of the children of men with compassion, forgiveness, and love. Solomon's temple has passed away. Scarce one stone is left upon another. But this great prayer, that made the hearts of the people beat as one man's in the unison of general confession and praise, remains a monument more lasting than brass or marble, testifying to the faith of the temple builders, and handing on to succeeding generations the contagion of a high courage and a hope which rests upon the compassion of the Eternal.

There are other moments in the history of the Jewish Church which "jut through oblivion's sea, like peaks of some sunk continent," moments made immortal by great petitions coming from the nation and its representatives, whether king or prophet, in the hour of some tragic experience followed by signal deliverance. The insolent blasphemies of Rabshakeh, messenger of Sennacherib, have brought Hezekiah and his people face to face with God, and together they have cried "O Lord our God, save us out of his hand." Why? "That all the kingdoms on earth may know that Thou art the Lord God, and Thou only." And ever and again in the history of those who put their trust in God, man's extremity is His opportunity. In that hour of sore need, Isaiah brings God's answer to Sennacherib, "The daughter of Zion hath despised thee, and laughed thee to scorn; the daughter of Jerusalem hath shaken her head at thee." The prayer of the nation is answered, and " all the kingdoms on earth " learn who is God.

The teachings of Jesus in His brief ministry have given a new meaning and purposes **Prayer in** to prayer. "If two or three of you shall **the Early** agree to ask anything as touching My **Church** Kingdom, it shall be done unto you." We may

ask for our daily bread, but the first objects of
our prayers must be the hallowing of His name,
the bringing in of His Kingdom, the doing of His
will. It is for these three ends that the hundred
and twenty in the upper room asked and received
"power from on high."

The Church thus called into being for the
redemption of the world remained effective for
its high calling so long as, and on condition that,
it was truly a praying Church. When threatened
with persecution, because Peter and John had
claimed that the lame man sitting for alms at the
Gate Beautiful of the Temple had been healed
"by the name of the crucified Jesus Christ of
Nazareth," the Church met for prayer, and again
the Holy Ghost came upon them and they defied
persecution and "spake the word of God with
boldness."

When compelled by the growth of the Church to
appoint deacons to take some of the burdens from
the shoulders of the Apostles, "they gave themselves continually to prayer," and the Word of God
increased, even "a great company of priests"
becoming "obedient unto the faith."

Again, it is when the Church is gathered together
to "minister" to the Lord by "prayer and fasting"
that the Holy Ghost says: "Separate me Barnabas
and Saul for the work of the ministry."

Still praying and fasting, the Church gives

their great commission to these two men. Supported by such prayers "they wax bold" and turn from the Jews, who rejected their message, and declare them to be unworthy of everlasting life, and Saul becomes Paul the Apostle of the Gentiles, an event second to few in the history of religion. That amazing apostolate "in labours more abundant, in prisons more frequent, in deaths oft" is sustained by the sympathy of a young Church in many lands which obeys his injunction, "Pray without ceasing."

Four centuries of the new era passed away. The Galilean had conquered. The Cross had taken the place of the Eagle as the standard **St. Benedict** of Empire. Constantine had declared **and Prayer** that his army shall fight henceforth *in hoc signo*. But temporal power had robbed the Church of so much that the accessions to its ranks of Emperors, Senators, and Consuls, were only Dead Sea apples. Victories, as judged by earthly standards, were too often defeats as Heaven sees them. Luxury and vice abounded amongst the followers of Jesus Christ, now patronised by the Emperor. Then it was that a young noble left Rome and all its comforts and pleasures for a cave at Subiaco. Here Benedict gathered others like-minded to pray that Christ might reign in their hearts, and the hearts of all men, as Lord and Master. The practice of religion in solitude by the Egyptian hermits was exchanged for the community life of the Western Church, and a new spirit entered the Church with the combined prayer and work of Benedict and his followers.

Those who saw this company of black-robed young men who had forsaken wealthy homes in Rome forty miles away to live on the gloomy mountain side, the chasm where lay the cave of Subiaco, by the daily toil of their hands, would have found it impossible to envisage where-unto this thing would grow, as impossible as for the townsman, who saw the children planting acorns and walnuts and chestnuts, to foresee without experience the forest that should result therefrom.

In three years' solitude Benedict had tested the hermit life, and for it he substituted the conception of a community whose religious life should be essentially social. No idle monks were they, but men "wearied with labours for God's sake." The Rule contains seventy-three chapters to guide the life of the Community. Thirteen regulate their worship of God, and of these, eleven are consecrated to those devotions which they held in common.

This group of young black-garbed Romans was to accomplish in its successors in the centuries that follow, the conversion of the Teutonic races and the civilisation of north-western Europe, and to

lay the foundations of education and culture in
many lands, preserving for us in its priceless libra-
ries the works of the great classical writers, as
well as those of the teachers of the Church.   They
were to provide Europe for generations with
missionaries, rulers, scholars, and teachers of
literature, science, and philosophy. All this sprang
directly from lives devoted to work and prayer.

Seven more centuries passed by, and the Church
had experienced many revivals, notably those of
Cluny in the tenth century, and Clair-
St. Bernard vaux in the twelfth century. The
and
St. Francis latter was associated with the name of
St. Bernard, whose passionate devotion
to our Lord finds expression in that great hymn
of love, "Jesu the very thought of Thee," sung
to-day by Christians of all communions. This
revival began when Bernard gathered round him
thirty young noblemen of Burgundy, who, in
corporate prayer, equipped themselves for service.
The high character of St. Bernard, his nobility
of nature, his wise charity, his tenderness in
dealing with others, and his genuine humility,
have compelled admiring tributes from men as
widely separated from him as Professor Alison
Phillips and T. Cotter Morison.

The thirteenth century is marked by the
evangelical revival of St. Francis. There is an
essential unity in the experience of Saul of Tarsus

when the Voice spoke to him on the road to
Damascus; of St. Francis in the Church of St.
Damian, when he knelt before the Crucifix and
realised the forgiveness of his sins; and of Wesley
on May the twenty-fourth, 1737, when, kneeling in
the room in Aldersgate Street, he "felt his heart
strangely warmed." There was much in common
between the twelve Penitents who made their
way from Assisi to Rome to obtain from Innocent
III sanction for the Order of Minorite Friars,
and the Holy Club at Oxford.

Francis and Wesley both had a devotion to
poverty, a passion for generous action towards
the needy and distressed of all kinds; and the
rapidity of the growth of the Franciscan movement
is parallel with that which marked the spread of
Methodism after Wesley's great experience.

In St. Luke's description of the events that
followed Pentecost, we read that striking passage
The Lucan in which he set out the quadrilateral
Quadri- of Christian practice which must mark
lateral the Church if it is to maintain the
spirit of Pentecost. "These all continued in the Apostles' doctrine." They had a
living experience of a personal Saviour. The
passage runs on: "And in the fellowship."
Fellowship is the inevitable outward expression
of unity of faith, unity in prayer, and unity in the
celebration of the love of our Lord in the Last

Supper. The "Breaking of the Bread" accompanies fellowship and united prayer. When Wesley had come to the last three months of his apostolate, his secret diary (a much more intimate document than the Journal written for publication) reveals to us how much the breaking of bread meant to him in those closing weeks of his life. On March 2nd, 1781, he died. We find in his diary that he received the Communion seven times in December, and nine times in January. We stand rebuked by this wonderful record of one in his 88th year. This was to him "the Trysting-place of Love."

Next in St. Luke's statement of the essentials of the Christian life are the Prayers. Here it is important to emphasise the fact that all forms of prayer have their own danger. Prayers nominally *ex tempore*, and printed prayers, may alike become stereotyped and barren. We may be charmed by the literary beauty of the legacy of prayers which a modern master of English has bequeathed to us, but in time this also loses its power. The same applies to many of the new litanies, living prayers that we hear on the broadcast. Frequent use will also make their repetition vain, unless they be inspired by a real sense of need and a living faith in the One to whom they are addressed. The prayer of Pentecost was imbued with the Spirit of the Cross, and the power of the Cross was shown in the changed lives of the thousands who that day were added to the Church. Prayer is a great task, lifting him who prays with the heart and with the understanding into the very Presence of God. The Practice of the Presence of God is the secret of essential and vital prayer. There are no easy tracks that lead us up to the Throne of God. Our Lord never offers His disciples the prize without the conflict, it must ever be a journey:

> " On with toil of heart and knees and hands
> Through the long gorge to the far light."

They who persevere will be sure of their reward. "To him that overcometh will I give to sit with Me on My Throne, even as I also overcame and am set down with My Father on His Throne." This promise is to each member of the Church, to all who bear the name of Christ, the whole Church. Again: "Ask and ye shall receive, Seek and ye shall find, Knock and it shall be opened unto you," is not only a promise to the individual, but a promise to the whole body of the faithful.

We must insist unceasingly that all Christians are called to be "Kings and Priests." None who have heard the call to service can fail to use the means which Jesus ordained without conscious disobedience. We cannot live lives separated from fellowship without that true schism which is a rending of the Body of Christ. "Because God Himself is eternal fellowship and eternal love, loneliness and selfishness cannot express Him." Our first fellowship in prayer must be at the family altar. There none will dispute the priestly duty and function of the head of the family. If this position be abdicated in the home, the wider circle of the Church or the nation will suffer. Therefore we are impelled to ask whether in many homes altars have never been built, or are broken down. We are driven by a great necessity to summon all Christian men to rebuild what is essential to the strength of the witness of the Church to our nation and to the world.

It is imperative that we should insist on "the breaking of bread" as the central occasion in the life of the Church for corporate prayer. In the passage quoted from St. Luke's account of Pentecost, these words are the link which unites fellowship and prayer. As Wesley's hymn expresses it:

> "This Eucharistic feast
> Our every want supplies."

This is the great occasion when, in the regular life of the Church, we are assured of "God's favour and goodness towards us, and that we are very members incorporate in the mystical body of His Son, which is the blessed company of all faithful people." This thought of fellowship, as associated

with the "breaking of bread," presents itself
again when St. Paul says, speaking of the institu-
tion of the Lord's Supper: "The cup of blessing
which we bless, is it not fellowship in the blood of
Christ, the bread which we break, is it not fellowship in the body of Christ, seeing that we who are
many are one bread, one body, for we all partake
of the one bread."

We must emphasise the fact that this great
fellowship, this Holy Communion, is not only
with all who, on earth, love our Lord Jesus Christ
in sincerity and truth. It is a fellowship with
quick and dead, "with angels and archangels and
all the Company of Heaven."

As we leave the table of our Lord, and meditate
on His command to do this in remembrance of
Him, we hear His voice across the ages saying to
us in our neglect of communion and fellowship
with Him, as He said to His three most trusted
disciples who had failed Him in the hour of His
need, "Could ye not watch with Me one hour?"
Gethsemane, with its agony and bloody sweat,
its travail for the souls of sinning men, its submission to the Divine Will, shames our negligence
and heedlessness of all He suffered for us, and our
disregard of His appeal to watch with Him, or,
in St. Paul's great phrase, "to fill up on our part
that which is lacking in the sufferings of Christ
for His Body's sake, which is the Church." The

eternal sacrifice of Calvary, ever continuing, repeats the message of Gethsemane, "the vesture keeps its bloody hue." That Sacred Body is still rent by our divisions, that Heart of Infinite Pity and Love is wounded afresh by our failure, those Feet that ever went about doing good, those Hands that ever ministered works of mercy, are pierced afresh when we fail to "watch with Him one hour." Bethany, with its promise of power to those who tarry, rebukes the inefficiency and impotence of our lives. Those days, crowded with happenings of supreme importance for the whole world, which began with the Supper in the upper room, and ended with the blessing on the Mount of Ascension, at every point summon us to unite with each other and to bring ourselves into union with our Lord in His great redemptive work.

By that Agony and Bloody Sweat, by that Cross and Passion, by that precious Death and Burial, by that glorious Resurrection and Ascension, by every hour from the Garden to the Mount of Ascension, we are summoned to watchfulness and prayer, to fellowship with our Lord in His sufferings and to unity with Him in His purpose.

This record of the treasury of devotion which has come down to us through the centuries is the chart of precious stores of spiritual treasures hidden, but easily found in the writings of the saints of each succeeding generation. On Carmel

and Olivet the Evangelists draw aside the veil
with inspired words that we may see the Trans-

**The Legacy
of the
Ages**
figuration and hear the colloquy of
the sinless Saviour with His Father, as
He gains strength from that communion to bear the sins of the world.
From the prisons of Imperial Rome; from the
solitary hermitages scattered along the sandy
banks of the Nile; from caves and castles under
the blue skies of Italy and Spain; from the home
of the Bishop of Geneva on the beautiful shores
of the Lake of Annecy; from the torture chambers
of the Inquisition; from the Tower of London;
from Bedford Jail; from the "Temples of Silence"
in Pennsylvania; from the little room in Aldersgate Street; from Oriel College and Hursley
Vicarage there comes an ever-growing stream of
testimony to the power of prayer, and an ever-
increasing volume of lessons by which our Lord
and His apostles of every age answer our cry,
"Teach us to pray."

Saint Augustine gives us in one bold and
memorable sentence the purpose of the Incarnation,
* *Factus est homo, ut homo fieret Deus* ("God was
made man, that man may be made God.") We
shall understand this striking saying better as we

---

* My attention has been called to the same thought
expressed earlier by St. Athanasius, "De Incarnatione"
54 Ἀυτὸς γαρ ἐνηιθρώπησεν, ἵνα ἡμεῖς θεοποιηθῶμεν.

listen to St. Paul's words, "I live, yet not I, but Christ liveth in me." Here is the goal which the saints have ever striven to reach—unity with God in His purpose, and to be "partakers of the Divine Nature." O Mystery of Mysteries! "The glory which Thou gavest Me, I have given them." This is the intention of our Lord for all who are members of the Mystical Body of Christ, that we may be more and more conformed to His Mind and Will, "and that we may all attain unto the unity of the faith, and of the knowledge of the Son of God, unto a full-grown man, unto the measure of the stature of the Fulness of Christ." This journey has been well defined as "an endless road along which we continue to advance." That advance is only assured by the grace that comes through the life of prayer, which therefore demands our close and constant study.

Chapter II

THE MASTERS OF MEDITATION

It may be helpful to begin this chapter on a personal note. It is thirty-five years since a friend first gave me the *Ignatian Exercises*. Four-and-twenty years have passed since I wrote the two little volumes, *The Love of Jesus* and *Retreats for the Soul*, and in the latter published a chapter on "Meditation" by the Rev. George Longridge, of the Community of the Resurrection. It is fifteen years since I was asked to speak at, and had the privilege of attending, a Conference on Retreats at Mirfield. On that occasion Father Longridge, of Cowley, expounded the Ignatian method of retreat and spoke on the "Exercises." It was not until I was preparing for the Committee on Corporate Prayer, appointed by the Wesleyan Methodist Conference of 1930, of which I was a member, and had drafted much that appears in the first chapter of this little book, that *The Art of Mental Prayer* by the Reverend Bede Frost, of the Anglican Benedictines, was given me for review, and I read and learned in a few days more about this great aid to the spiritual life than I had grasped in thirty-five years' previous consideration of the question. I make this confession with great regret that the years that have gone by were not strengthened and quickened by a more systematic and effective practice of this supremely important duty and privilege of the Christian life.

This ought not to have been so. John Wesley did his best to train his people in meditation.

John Wesley's insistence on meditation. I have just now in my hand a little duo-decimo volume, bound in leather, printed more than a century and a quarter ago, and published at the Conference Office, Finsbury Square. The volume is entitled *An Extract of the Christian's Pattern : or, A Treatise on the Imitation of Christ written in Latin by Thomas à Kempis, abridged and published in English by John Wesley, M.A.* Wesley, in his terse fashion, directs his people to read this book and meditate upon it. His directions are all worth quoting because they contain so much that is valuable on this question of Meditation, and with Wesley's honoured name will carry weight to his own people and to others who revere his apostolic ministry. He writes:—

"As it is impossible for any one to know the usefulness of this TREATISE, till he has read it in such a manner as it deserves: instead of heaping up commendations of it, which those who have so read it do not want, and those who have not, will not believe: I have transcribed a few plain directions how to read this (or indeed any other religious book) with improvement.

"1. Assign some stated time every day for this pious employment. If any indispensable business unexpectedly robs you of your hour of retirement, take the next hour for it: *When such large portions of each day are so willingly bestowed on bodily refreshments, can you scruple allotting some little time daily for the improvement of your immortal soul ?*

"2. Prepare yourself for reading by purity of intention, whereby you singly aim at your soul's benefit; and then, in a short ejaculation, beg God's grace to enlighten your understanding, and dispose your heart for receiving what you read; and, that you may both know what He requires of you, and seriously resolve to execute His will when known.

"3. Be sure to read, not curiously and hastily, but leisurely, seriously, and with great attention; with proper intervals and pauses, that you may allow time for the enlightenings of divine grace. Stop every now and then to recollect what you have read, and consider how to reduce it to practice. Further, let your reading be continued and regular, not rambling and desultory. It shews a vitiated palate, to taste of many dishes without fixing upon, or being satisfied with any; not but what it will be of great service to read over and over those passages, which more nearly concern yourself, and more closely affect your own practice or inclinations: especially if you add a particular examination upon each.

"4. Labour for a temper correspondent to what you read; otherwise it will prove empty and unprofitable, while it only enlightens your understanding, without influencing your will, or inflaming your affections. Therefore, intersperse here and there, pious aspirations to God, and petitions for His grace. Select also any remarkable sayings or advices, treasuring them up in your memory to ruminate and consider on: which you may either in time of need draw forth, as arrows from a quiver, against temptation, against this or that vice which you are more particularly addicted to; or make use of as incitements to humility, patience, the love of God, or any virtue.

"5. Conclude all with a short ejaculation to God; that He would preserve and prosper His good seed sown in your heart, that it may bring forth its fruit in due season. And think not this will take up too much of your time, for you can never bestow it to so good advantage."

Any one who faithfully follows the advice Wesley gives will graduate successfully in the art to which Wesley rightly attaches supreme importance. Let us now sit at the feet of some of the great teachers in this school during the earlier centuries of the Church's history.

St. Augustine—perhaps the greatest of all the Masters of Meditation—was God's gift to the Church at a time when the spiritual vigour of the Church's life was first seriously threatened by the patronage of the civil power. Augustine was great from every standpoint—the gifts of nature, the opportunities of high service, and the achievements of a long and honoured life. He was the greatest of the four Latin fathers of the Church—"more profound than Ambrose, his spiritual father, more original and systematic than Jerome, his correspondent, and of much greater intellectual power than Gregory the Great, his pupil on the papal throne." There is no name since the apostolic age which has exercised such power over the Christian Church, no mind that has so deeply impressed its thought. Dom Butler, in the striking study of Saint Augustine, which is found in his "Western Mysticism," does not exaggerate when he says that Augustine is the Prince of Mystics, uniting in himself in a manner not found in any other, "the two elements of mystical experience, viz. the most penetrating

Augustine
Born Nov. 13, 354
Died Aug. 28, 430

intellectual vision into things divine, and a love
of God that was a consuming passion. He shines
as a sun in the firmament, shedding forth at
once light and heat in the lustre of his intellect and
the warmth of his religious emotion."

And this master intellect was led, in the
providence of God, to throw open, in his Confessions, the doors of his most sacred chamber, that
all mankind might know the full story of his sins,
of his philosophic doubts and wanderings, of the
Grace of God that followed him with a persistence
even greater than his mother's love, of his conversion and of the revelation to his soul of the
power and majesty and purpose of the Eternal.
The Confessions of Saint Augustine is one of the
greatest books of all time, and is unsurpassed
as a guide in the realm of the spirit. In our
endeavours to learn the secrets of the Saints, we
can scarcely spend too long in the home of Augustine and his mother Monica. The *Confessions*
are vital to our study because they provide the
greatest examples of prayers in the history of the
Christian Church. Here we have one long
conversation with God, one unbroken colloquy
with Him; every sentence is addressed directly
to Him.

In these pages we seek to emphasize the contemplative life in which Augustine communicates
with God. Nevertheless, we must not fail to

remember that Augustine always lays his emphasis
upon the prevenience of the Grace of God. He
seeks in prayer and meditation to lay hold upon
Him, but he never forgets that his life is an
answer to a divine act, and this great fact regulates
all his spiritual life. "Thou wast at the helm,
but very secretly."

This continuous prayer, which gives such
emphasis to St. Paul's injunction "pray without
ceasing," equals in volume the total length of the
four Gospels, the Acts, and the Epistle to the
Romans. Its value is intensified by the fact that
every word is written in the conscious presence of
God, as one long meditation, with many petitions
embedded in it. Here indeed is a master who
teaches us from his own experience how to meditate
and how to pray.

And it is from Augustine that we learn with
emphasis the lesson that St. Paul has already
taught, that the only possibility of progress on
the path towards union with God is by spiritual
discipline. At the same time the great principle
is insisted upon that it is possible in this life to
have the Vision of God—experimental perceptions
of Him. The lesson (of the Gospel) is clearly
taught that it is the pure in heart who see God,
that purgation must precede illumination. We
here learn the vital lesson that there is no conflict
between the discipline of love and the doctrine of

justification by faith.   Augustine had entered into
an experience similar to that of St. Paul, when he
burst out with his exultant words "there is therefore now no condemnation to them that are in Christ
Jesus," with Luther when he realised that "the
just shall live by faith," and with Wesley when
there came to him the consciousness of the testimony of the Holy Spirit in his heart that nevertheless he was a child of God.   He teaches us that the
indispensable condition of spiritual growth is such
a purification of the soul as will render it fit for the
ascent to the contemplation of God.

Augustine's *Confessions* are the more impressive
because they appeal to the man of affairs, since
he was in many ways the greatest of that class
which has been styled "Practical Mystics."   His
other masterly work, *The City of God*, in which
he strove to build a spiritual kingdom upon the
ruins of the old Roman Empire, gives us the following definition of "The two lives, the active and
the contemplative."   "The study and pursuit of
wisdom lies in action and in contemplation so that
one part of it may be called 'active' and the
other 'contemplative.'   The active is concerned
with living one's life and moral conduct; the contemplative with beholding the causes of nature
and most pure truth."   The busy man who turns
from a crowded life to find help from these *Confessions*, will be encouraged by the fact that

although Augustine recognises that in the story of Martha and Mary, Martha chose a good part, and Mary chose the better, he does definitely teach, "Martha's part is holy and great." Both are praiseworthy, but the one is laborious, the other leisured. "What Martha was doing, there we are; what Mary, that we hope for. While in this life how much can we have of Mary's part? For even now we do somewhat of her work, when removed from businesses and laying aside our ordinary cares. Inasmuch as we do thus, we are like to Mary."

It will help us greatly to pass again and again over the rich field of spiritual treasure contained in the *Confessions*, and to gather some of the nuggets and jewels of eternal value lying on the surface, which shall enrich us, as others in generation after generation have been enriched thereby. Half-way through the volume, in the Tenth Book, Augustine utters this unparalleled confession in the sight of all men and for all time, "With what fruit therefore, O Lord my God—to whom my conscience confesseth daily, being more secure in the hope of Thy mercy than in the consideration of mine own innocency—with what fruit, I beseech Thee, shall I in Thy presence, by this writing confess even to men, not only what I have been, but even what now I am. . . . And will they pray for me, when they shall understand how

much I am held down by the weight of my sins?
To such men as this will I discover myself. For it
is no small fruit, O Lord my God, that Thou
mayst both be thanked by many, and prayed to
by many, on my behalf. Let the brotherly mind
love that in me which Thou teachest us to love,
and grieve for that which Thou teachest us to
grieve for.''

These passages must suffice to show the sufficient
reasons which impelled Augustine to throw aside
all reserve that he might help others toward that
vision which was his supreme joy.

The book opens—as any meditation or
prayer may well do—with a burst of adoration
and praise. "Great art Thou, O Lord, and greatly
worthy to be praised; great is Thy power, and of
Thy wisdom there is no end." Through four
chapters Augustine thinks aloud, to help his
readers to realise the Supremacy, the Justice, the
Power, the Mercy, the Beauty, and the Un-
changeableness of God. He longs that God
should enter "the house of his soul," but it is
"too strait," and he prays that it may be en-
larged. To this end he recites the mercies of
God which began in infancy and have ever continued. Then follows that amazing confession
in which he acknowledges to God the stirrings of
sin in his heart from childhood onwards, leading
on through the sins of youth to early manhood,

which only fails to repel us because we know that we are permitted to witness the humbling of a great soul before God that we may be led, by his example, to the like saving humility and to press on to the same goal. His "hatred of the Greek language" perplexes him, and he is distressed that "the delicacy of the fabled stories" of Homer should thus have been "sprinkled with gall." He deplores the stories he reads "of Jupiter the thunderer and adulterer," and apostrophises as "a flood of hell" the "promises of reward that induce men to learn these things." "What marvel," he asks, "was it if I were thus carried towards vanity and estranged from Thee, O my God?" The literary training which taught him "not to use barbarisms of speech," was the means of his falling into "a deep pit of filth." The twentieth chapter, ending the first book of his confessions, closes on the note that whilst in his youth he "had rushed headlong upon sorrow, confusion and error," yet "I give Thee thanks for all Thy gifts, my Delight, my Glory, my Confidence and my God." Thus are we taught how we may be borne nearer to God by a meditation on, and a recital of, our sins and the mercies of God in the days of our youth.

One cannot, unfortunately, within the limits of these pages, continue a detailed study of the methods of Augustine in meditation and prayer. Deeply interesting is the story of his wanderings into the errors of the Manicheans, the passionate love of his mother, Monica, and the comforting words of the old bishop to her, "Go thy ways and God bless thee, it is impossible that the son of these tears should perish." The ultimate answer to these prayers is told in the well-known story of his conversion in the garden when the voice spake to him and said "Take up and read." There is a strange compelling power in the words with which he leads up to the climax of his story and says, "Now I will declare and confess Thy name, O Lord, my Helper and my Redeemer, in what manner Thou didst free me from the chain of sensual desires which so straitly bound me."

His account of his last conversation with his mother in spiritual things is full of instruction. She had loved him so passionately, and cared for him and her family "as if she had been the mother of us all; and yet she did so serve us, as if she had been the daughter of us all." The time came when she was to depart out of this life, and by God's special guidance he and she were left alone. "There did we confer with much dear tenderness, and, forgetting those things which are behind, we reached forth unto those things which are before, we did enquire between ourselves of Thee, who art the ever-present Truth, of what kind should be that eternal life of the saints in heaven, which the eye hath not seen, nor the ear heard, nor hath it entered into the heart of man. . . . And then we struck inward upon the consideration of our own souls, and did even transcend and pass beyond them also, that we might touch upon the confines of that region of plenty which never faileth, where Thou feedest Israel from all eternity with the food of Truth, and where Life is that very Wisdom of Thine, by which all these things both are, and were, and shall be made." We have here and in the passages that follow, a wonderful illustration of the way in which we may draw nearer to each other and nearer to God in Christian fellowship, and how the joy of solitary meditation may be transcended by the help that comes when two souls are able, in Augustine's words, "to take a little taste with the whole force of our hearts." Even in silence the communion was great, and then, he says, "We returned again to the noise of language, where every word is begun and ended." On this he makes the striking comment, "How little like to Thy Word, our Lord, who remaineth in Himself without length of days, and yet reneweth all things!"

The Secret of the Confessions of St. Augustine is also that of Brother Lawrence's *Practice of the Presence of God*. The humble lay brother in the kitchen, and the great Doctor of the Church in his study, found the solution of all the problems of life in this intimate communion with God.

Everything in both lives was laid bare before Him. No failure was too small to be confessed to Him. No trial was so light that its burden might not be cast upon Him. And thus was created a complete intimacy of the human soul with the Divine, that brought the power of heaven down to the weakness of earth, that equipped mortal helplessness with the might of the Eternal for every conflict of Life.

The later chapters of the *Confessions* are given to meditations on the great problems of the Universe—Time, Space, Eternity, Infinity, Heaven and the Angels, Hell and the Devils. God was equally near to the Philosopher and to the Servitor, and this great book is brought to its close with a prayer for the peace of the Eternal Sabbath, "a peace without an evening." All other days had both a morning and an evening, "but the seventh day hath no evening, nor hath it any setting because Thou hast sanctified it to continue everlastingly. . . . We also shall rest in Thee, in the Sabbath of life eternal."

As we pass to the consideration of the life and teaching of Bernard of Clairvaux, we are conscious of a great change of spiritual atmosphere and temperature. Not only is it true, as Etienne Gilson says, "St. Bernard is not merely a mystic, but a pure mystic, without any trace of philosophy about him," but it is also true, as

Bernard of Clairvaux, 1090–1153.

is pointed out by Dom Butler, that the mysticism of St. Augustine, "the Prince of Mystics," begins from a different starting point in his experiences when he was first influenced by the books of the Platonists and tells us, "I entered and beheld with the eye of my soul the Light Unchangeable," and adds "I trembled with love and awe." On this Dom Butler comments: "There is a special interest in the circumstances that these experiences, evidently in full sense mystical, were pre-Christian, or at any rate pre-Catholic. He did not yet accept the Catholic doctrine of the Incarnation or the divinity of Christ." Augustine had a supreme consciousness of the majesty and power of God, which has characterised his followers both within and without the Church of Rome. Bernard is "the Master Innovator of the Middle Ages." As Pere Rousselot puts it, "The great novelty, the incomparable value of the medieval religion is an understanding and love, or rather a passion, for the Humanity of Christ; the Incarnate Word. *Homo Christus Jesus* is not merely the Model to be imitated, the Guide to be followed, or from another point of view, the Uncreated Light which illumines the depths of the soul; He is also the Spouse of the soul, her Fellow-Worker and her Friend." The following lines indicate the striking novelty of Bernard's teaching, and his intimacy with Jesus— "I salute Thee, my beloved Jesus! I desire

always to cling to Thy Cross, and Thou knowest
why. Come to my aid. Look down upon me
from Thy Cross, O Beloved of my soul, draw me
all to Thyself, only say to me: 'I will heal thee and
I forgive thee all.' Inflamed with Thy love and
overwhelmed with shame, I embrace Thee, and I
cling to Thee. Oh, Thou knowest only too well
the reason, but bear with me and say nothing
and be not displeased with my boldness." Père
Rousselot continues: "No more is necessary to
show that this is indeed a 'new song.' We are
as far removed here from Prudentius and St.
Ambrose as from Virgil. Antiquity had never
thus joined to a humility deep and heart-rending,
so simple, familiar and burning a love. At one
and the same moment he recognises, in Him Who
hangs upon the Cross, his Brother and his God."

St. Bernard's great exposition of the Song of
Solomon, expressed so frequently in the language
of human love, has been criticised by Dean Inge
and others. It is, however, important to note
that for St. Bernard it is the Church that is
primarily the Bride. The Bridegroom is the
Divine Word, called more than once "the Bridegroom Word." The following extract taken from
his last sermon on the Canticle reveals at once his
sublime thought, his fervent devotion and his
great eloquence. It does, however, identify the
soul with the Bride: "The return of the soul is its

conversion, that is, its turning to the Word. . . . It loves Him as it is loved by Him. And if this love is perfected, the soul is wedded to the Word. What can be more full of happiness and joy than this conformity? What more to be desired than this love, which makes thee, O soul, no longer content with human guidance, to draw near with confidence thyself to the Word, to attach thyself with constancy to Him, to address Him familiarly and consult Him upon all subjects, to become as receptive in thy intelligence as fearless in thy desires?"

In another passage he contrasts God as the Father and Christ as the Bridegroom. He says, "What other bond or constraining force do you seek for between spouses than to be loved and to love? . . . God says: If I be Father, where is My honour? He says that as a Father. But if He declares Himself to be a Bridegroom, will He not change the word and say: If I be Bridegroom, where is My love? For He had previously said: If I be Lord, where is My fear? God, then, requires that He should be feared as Lord, honoured as Father, but as Bridegroom loved. Which of these three is highest and most to be preferred? Surely it is love. Love, then, is a great reality."

Such passages as these reveal to us the loving devotion of St. Bernard to the Sacred Humanity.

It is interesting to note that St. Francis of Assisi (who a century later taught the same passionate devotion to our Lord, though, as is justly remarked, he had probably never read anything of St. Bernard's writings,) left disciples, notably St. Bonaventura, who owe much to St. Bernard. The whole school of the Franciscans is influenced by St. Bernard's teaching on devotion to "the Sacred Humanity of our Lord." "Augustine is lost in wonder over the humiliations of the Word: Bernard grows tender over the cries and the frailty of the 'Little One, the Desire of all little ones.'"

St. Bernard, in his "new song," brings us through Christ the Man to Christ who is God.

St. Bernard is another striking illustration of the power of the mystic in practical affairs, of the fact that devotion to our Lord and intimate communion with Him is a source of strength for dealing with the problems of life. Cotter Morison, the agnostic who has written so remarkable a biography of Bernard, says, "looking back on Bernard through a vista of seven centuries, he appears as one of the great active minds of his age—commanding kings, compelling nations, influencing and directing the men and things among which he lived—in a word, one of the statesmen of history. And in truth he was all this. The twelfth century would have had another aspect

if he had never lived." This activity was an
accident, added on to his true career which he
had chosen for himself, to be a prayerful monk,
working out his own salvation with fear and
trembling. A very interesting tribute comes
from Cotter Morison when he refers to the remote-
ness of some of Bernard's sermons from the
attitude of to-day. He says "Not only his system
and philosophy, but half-a-dozen other systems and
philosophies, which have supplanted his and each
other, have been cast aside as valueless since he
lived." Nevertheless, he goes on to argue that
"it is not long ago that many a grand old Gothic
cathedral was ridiculed, even despised for its
quaint gargoyles and portals," and he asks to be
allowed the argument that some of the antique
solemnity and massiveness of twelfth-century
aisles and choirs will be found in Bernard's
sermons, which once awakened such widespread
religious echoes. We may well get back to his
spirit of passionate devotion to the "Sacred
Humanity of our Lord," and we shall find that by
so doing we shall not lose touch with the realities
of the life of to-day.

Bernard's conversion took place, as he tells us
in graphic terms, in a wayside church as he
"poured forth his heart like water" (*effundens
sicut aquam cor suum*) "in the presence of his
Lord." From that moment commenced a life

of stern discipline, a resolute determination to detach himself at once from the temptations and from the cares of the world. As so often has happened in the lives of great saints and mystics, such separation proved his fitness for dealing with the affairs of State and Church, and equipped him for a life of great activity. He joined the reformed Benedictine Order of Cistercians, a rule which might have seemed severe enough. They commenced with private prayer for two hours, matins, to which the monks were summoned at two, and the next common service began with the first glimmer of dawn, the interval being spent in Cloister, in reading, writing and meditation. Work in the fields from 9 till 2, when the one meal of the day was taken; Vespers at sunset. The day finished with prayers. And yet such austerities were inadequate to satisfy his zeal. What he insisted was the duty of all Christians during Holy Week in his great sermon on the Passion of our Lord, he applied to himself for every moment of his life. "Cultivate holiness, follow out humility, put on gravity, suffer with Christ's sufferings." "Happy ye to suffer, that ye may suffer on account of the Son of God," says St. Bernard in the spirit in which St. Paul exclaimed, "I fill up on my part that which is lacking in the sufferings of Christ." "Our Lord Jesus Christ has embraced us through our labour and pain;

let us also embrace Him with corresponding
returns on account of His righteousness, and according to His righteousness. Feed us meanwhile,
Lord, with the bread of tears, until Thou lead us
to a good measure, full and heaped up, which
Thou shalt pour into our bosoms, who art in the
bosom of the Father, above all, God blessed for
evermore." With such passionate pleadings did
he urge a life of complete renunciation upon his
fellows, and with such ardour did he manifest his
love for Christ, in stern discipline and a with-
drawal from the world which the world itself
thought a strange preparation for the active life
that was to follow.

It is not possible in these pages to do more than
glance at all that the thirteenth and fourteenth
centuries have to tell us of the open
**The Friends
of God.** secret of the Saints in the records of
St. Francis and his followers, and St.
Dominic and the Friars who bore his name. Speaking of these great leaders and some of their
followers we may well say that they had "a passion
for our Saviour's Passion." Devotion to the
Sacred Humanity crucified for us, is the key-
note of the life of Bonaventura the Franciscan,
and later on of Savonarola the Dominican, manifested in his *Treatise on the Love of Jesus*.

The fourteenth century was marked by a movement
of reform under the name "The New

Devotion," which was influenced by the mystic speculations of Ruysbroeck and Suso and Tauler. We trace the continuation of St. Bernard's characteristic devotion in the teaching of Bonaventura. At the Grindelwald Conference of 1894, we were startled when Professor Lindsay, historian of the Reformation, father of the present Master of Balliol, told us of a gathering of "The Friends of God," as they were called, that took place in that same valley five centuries earlier. He called it "an earlier Reunion Conference at Grindelwald," to which Nicholas of Basle, the great "Friend of God," from the Bernese Oberland, brought "his followers, John Tauler, the great mystic, Rulman Merswin, banker in Strasbourg, Henry Suso, and Christiana Ebner, prioress of the Convent at Ulm," and letters were read, among others, from the sainted Queen of Hungary. Dr. Lindsay claimed for these "Friends of God" that they "prayed for the Reformation, and that what they themselves were unable to do, God did for them through their prayers before a hundred years were over." Père Deniflé, the critic of Luther, has objected to the statement that these men were the forerunners of the Reformation. This is not a controversial work, and it must suffice to point out how much the devotional life of Christendom gained from this Grindelwald group of the "Friends of God," influenced as they were by the teaching of the two great mystics, Ruysbroeck and Eckhart. To use the striking phrase of Baron von Hügel, "One torch lights another torch," and these souls aflame with love for Christ handed on their passion to succeeding generations, through channels which we can all recognise. One of the "Friends of God," a priest, wrote in German, about the year 1350, the well-known book *Theologia Germanica*, or *The Book of the Perfect Life*. Luther, who first published this remarkable book in 1516 or 1518, says that he owed more to it than any other book, excepting the Bible and St. Augustine. Professor Vernet, of Lyons University, nevertheless says that this work is not a manifesto in favour of Lutheranism or of Pantheism, but that from his standpoint as a Roman Catholic historian, it is perfectly orthodox. The following passage from the Thirteenth Chapter gives us the characteristic point of view of the writer:—

"Tauler saith: 'There be some men at the present time, who take leave of types and symbols too soon, before they have drawn out all the truth and instruction contained therein.' Hence they are scarcely or perhaps never able to understand the truth aright. For such men will follow no one, and lean unto their own understandings, and desire to fly before they are fledged. They would fain mount up to heaven in one flight; albeit

Christ did not so, for after His resurrection, He remained full forty days with His beloved disciples. No one can be made perfect in a day.   A man must begin by denying himself, and willingly forsaking all things for God's sake, and must give up his own will, and all his natural inclinations, and separate and cleanse himself thoroughly from all sins and evil ways.   After this, let him humbly take up the cross and follow Christ."

The next chapter describes the purgative, illuminative, and unitive ways of advance in the spiritual life.

The *New Devotion* of these "Friends of God" centres around the person of Christ.   It is not only the Christ of Bethlehem and Calvary, but also of Nazareth and the public life.   Christ is the Model of life from day to day.   Therefore, the *New Devotion* finds its fullest manifestation in Thomas Hemmerken, born at Kempen in the diocese of Cologne, who will be known as long as Christendom endures, under the name of Thomas à Kempis.   Writing a century later than Tauler and Ruysbroeck, he was definitely under their influence.   Tauler had published a notable sermon entitled "Imitation of the Life of Poverty of Our Lord Jesus Christ," and the glory of Thomas à Kempis lies above all in his *Imitation of Christ*. This book appeared in the very centre of the influences of the *New Devotion*, and the spirit of that movement is well expressed in the passage: "Nothing is sweeter than love, nothing more courageous, nothing higher, nothing wider, nothing more pleasant, nothing fuller nor better in Heaven and earth; because Love is born of God, and cannot rest but in God, above all created things." That great chapter in *The Imitation*, "Of the Royal Way of the Holy Cross," gives perfect expression to the passionate devotion to the crucified Christ, which characterised both St. Bernard and *The New Devotion*. "Behold! in the Cross all doth consist, and all lieth in our dying thereon: for there is no other way unto life, and unto true inward peace, but the way of the Holy Cross."

It is not surprising that the student of history should find that in the Age of Chivalry women **Women Leaders in Devotion.** play a leading part, not only in religious affairs, but also in temporal matters. It is impossible to parallel outside the Roman Communion the activities and the influences of Saint Catherine of Siena and Saint Catherine of Genoa and Saint Teresa, until the nineteenth century, when Elizabeth Fry, Florence Nightingale, Josephine Butler, and Catherine Booth scattered the conventions of Protestantism and opened up spheres of service for Christ and for humanity which had been closed for generations.

When Hugh Price Hughes founded his Sisterhood of the People, he deliberately chose that name to parallel St. Vincent de Paul's "Little Sisters of the Poor," but his courage failed when I suggested that the lady who, during his lifetime, and for a generation afterwards, served that Sisterhood as its head with such devotion, should be called the Reverend Mother Superior. Her life has been inspired by the same passion for holiness and passion for humanity that marked the lives of the Saints of Siena and Genoa, whose name she bore. Few women in the history of the Universal Church have more fully deserved to be called "Reverend Mother."

We have much to learn from these three women, the two Catherines and Teresa. Saint Catherine of Siena was born on 25th March, 1347, exactly a century and a quarter after the death of that great mystic, Francis of Assisi, and died in April, 1380. In her thirty-three years she accomplished work which remains the marvel of all students, both in the political and in the religious sphere. Prevented by her friends from entering any religious order, excepting as a tertiary of the Dominican Order, she faced in the busy life of home duties the inevitable difficulty of securing time for private prayer. In these circumstances she withdrew herself into what she called "the little cell of the heart," and cultivated personal communion with Christ with a passionate ardour, which, as her biographer, Mr. Gardner, has well said, is "repulsive to the eyes of many in an age that worships material gain and physical comfort." She paralleled St. Paul's statement "How often could I have wished myself accursed from Christ for my brethren" by saying, "How could I be content, Lord, if any one of those who have been created in Thy image and likeness, even as I, should perish and be taken out of Thy hands? . . . Better were it for me that all should be saved, and I alone should sustain the pains of hell, than that I should be in paradise and they all perish damned." To use her own words, "As the fountain of all her life she set, as against self-love, the stone of self-knowledge, which she distinguished into three small stones: the first the consideration of Creation, the second the consideration of Redemption, and the third the consideration of her own sins."

She tells how, after praying for strength, she received this message from God, "Daughter, if thou wouldst acquire the virtue of fortitude, thou must needs imitate Me. . . . If thou wouldst become strong to overcome every power of the enemy, take the Cross for thy consolation, even as I did, who, as My Apostle says, having joy set before Me, endured the Cross."

It is outside the purpose of these pages to speak

at any length of her plunge into political life. It is only possible to emphasise the lesson that here again the practical mystic showed the power of spiritual gifts to equip her for work in temporal affairs. Her courage when she wrote to the Pope, Cardinals, Bishops, and others, astounds us when we remember that she was only a young girl with no influence or political standing. To Pope Gregory, for instance, she writes bidding him in the name of Christ Crucified to extirpate the evil pastors and rulers, "full of impurity and cupidity, puffed up with pride." Later on she writes of the Cardinals who were playing false to Pope Urban, and addresses them as "Fools worthy of a thousand deaths." She tells them "On whatever side I turn I find in you nothing save lies." It is only possible again to emphasise the fact that the power of this marvellous life was due to her retreat into "the little cell of the heart." Of this she says, writing to one who, like herself, was immersed in affairs, "you will seldom be able to have an actual cell, but I would have you always dwell in the cell of the heart, and always bear it with you. For, as you know, when we are locked into that, our enemies cannot offend us. Then every exercise that you do will be directed and ordained by God."

Saint Catherine of Genoa (1447–1510) has been deservedly enshrined in Baron von Hügel's monumental work, *The Mystical Element of Religion*, as studied in her life, which is a priceless contribution to our knowledge of God and the Transcendent Love. St. Catherine's is another case of a life lived entirely outside of the customary conventual life to which most women of deep religious convictions were devoted in her age. Her conversion, at the age of sixteen, was as definite an event as that of the conversion of Saul of Tarsus. Her heart was pierced by so sudden and immense a love of God, that in a transport of pure and all-purifying love, she kept crying within herself "No more world, no more sin." Some of those that have written her life have held that the usual lengthy and succeeding effects of the purgative, illuminative, and unitive experiences were achieved in her case in the one moment of her conversion. The fact is, that for the remaining thirty-seven years of her life, her interior history represents one continuous widening, deepening and moving onwards of effort, trial and faith, of achievements and ideals. There was no limit to the devotion with which Catherine threw herself into the work she undertook, the charge during the plague of a large hospital with 136 beds. Determined to master all her squeamishness in this, her lowly work, she cleansed the houses of the Hospital from disgusting filth, took home with her the garments of the poor, covered with dirt and vermin, and cleansed them before returning them to their owners. Speaking of her labours during that pestilential outbreak, von Hügel says, "Beautiful, utterly self-oblivious impulsiveness; a sleepless sense of the omnipresence of Christ as Love, and of this Love filling all things that aspire and thirst after it, as spontaneously as the liberal air and the overflowing mother's breast fill and feed even the but slightly aspiring or the painfully labouring lungs and the eager, helpless infant mouth; swift, tender, warm, whole-hearted affection for this outwardly poor and disfigured, but inwardly rich and beautiful fellow-creature and twin-vessel of election; an underlying virile ecstaticity of perseverance and strenuous, cheerful, methodical, laboriousness; all these things are clearly there."

Santa Teresa of Cepeda (1515–1582), the third of these saintly women, was born a few years after the death of Saint Catherine of Genoa. She became a nun at eighteen, but was only consciously converted at forty. As her mystical visions were criticised severely while she lived, and have been criticised many times since, it may be well to quote what her biographer, Mrs. Cunningham-Grahame, says: "No one born was less hysterical than Teresa. Her life was calm, orderly, full of discipline; her actions free from precipitation and haste; her mind clear, shrewd and sharp. And this same clearness, sharpness, shrewdness, is as discernible in her relation of a vision as in her narrative of the foundation of a convent." She did not enter on her great life's work until she was forty-five years of age, and then she set herself the task of founding convents of Reformed Carmelites all over Spain. After her great second Divine "Locution," or vision, she wrote with a ring of triumph in her words: "Let all the learned men rise up against me, let all created things persecute me, let devils torment me, but do not Thou fail me, Lord, for I know the gain which Thou deliverest to him who alone confides in Thee. . . ." There was justification for these strong words, as many critics within the Church would like to have proved her to be a heretic. Those were the days when heresy in Spain was eagerly sought out and severely punished. Even St. John of the Cross, the great apostle who shared her labours, did not escape suspicion, and Ignatius Loyola himself was thrown into prison at Salamanca. From these facts we gain some idea of the way in which Teresa's visions were first received. Facing with great courage the petty and irritating martyrdoms to which she was now exposed, she could afford to disregard the threats of exorcism as she was absorbed in visions so radiant that one of them was worth more than all the treasures and pleasures the world could give.

It is easy to understand Bishop Gore's statement that her experiences would have furnished Baron von Hügel with a marvellous field of study. Her first revelation caused her celebrated vow of perfection, the Teresian vow, or the "Seraphic Vow" which the Church affirmed afterwards to be taught by God, and which she religiously kept for five years of her life. The resolution was "Not to do anything that she, or those about her, did not understand to be most perfect." The secret of the life of Saint Teresa is revealed in the following passage from Chapter XXX of her book, *The Way of Perfection*:—

"St. Augustine tells us that after searching for a long time to find God in the things that surrounded him, he discovered Him at last within himself. Meditate deeply these words, for it is of great profit for anyone that has difficulty in recollecting himself to understand this truth; to know that it is not necessary for him to raise himself to Heaven in order to converse with his Divine Father and find his happiness with Him, nor to elevate his voice so as to be heard; God is so near that He hears the slightest whisper from our lips and the most secret thought. We have no need of wings to go in search of Him; let us enter into the solitude and look within us, it is there that He is. Let us talk with Him in great humility, but also with love, like children talking with their Father, confidently

telling Him our troubles and begging Him to help
us, and recognising above all that we are not
worthy to bear the name of His children.''

These three saintly women differed widely in
character. No greater contrast could be imagined
than the life of service and love for the poor and
disinherited in the slums of Genoa, and in the
plague-stricken streets of that Italian city, as
compared with the visits of Catherine of Sienna to
Avignon, with all its luxury and corruption, or the
long journeys over the mountains of Spain which
Santa Teresa accomplished in her apostolic
labours as she went about from place to place
establishing convents of those who had accepted
her severe rule in protest against the laxity of the
religious orders of her day. These women were
one in their absolute devotion to their Lord, in
their complete spirit of self-renunciation, the
renunciation which can only come from a passionate love for a Person, and in their aspiration after
complete union between Christ and His Apostles
which enabled St. Paul to say: "I live, yet not I,
but Christ liveth in me." In like manner, to these
three great mystics there was given the sense of
espousal to Christ, of becoming the bride of Christ,
of complete union with Christ which furnished the
basis of all their activities in the world their
presence blessed and inspired. They proved
beyond controversy that a life of constant

prayer will also be a life of most effective service.

The secret of the saints, revealed in the lives of Lancelot Andrewes, Jeremy Taylor and Thomas Wilson, Bishops of the Church of Eng-**Three Post-** land after the Reformation, differs no **Reformation** whit from that which we have learnt **Anglican** **Bishops.** from the lives we have just studied.

They were all pilgrims looking for the same " city, which hath foundations, whose builder and maker is God." Bishops in England, Ireland, and the Isle of Man, they spoke the same spiritual language as the Bishop of Hippo, the Abbot of Clairvaux, and the German Mystics.

The uprising of national Churches in Northern Europe during the sixteenth century, and the revolt against the supremacy of Rome, were marked by many tragedies, but did not alter the summons to Christians in every country to be saints, or prevent a real unity in Christ. On the plains below man might differ and fight, but on the Mount of Transfiguration our Lord, and Moses and Elijah worked out the great synthesis of the Gospel, the Law and the Prophets, and there was no need for "three tabernacles." The Apostle who suggested this, as St. Mark tells us, "wist not what to say, for he was sore afraid." So is it ever, in that blessed intimacy with our Lord division becomes impossible. Far above the cries of suffering humanity, in that

> "Ampler, purer air,
> Above the stir of toil and care,"

those who enter into fellowship with our Lord are one in spirit.

Lack of space has prevented us in this review from dealing with those great British Mystics, Richard Rolle of Hampstead, Dame Julian of Norwich, and the author of *The Cloud of Unknowing*, or with many after the Reformation, the Cambridge Platonists, William Law and others, the contribution of the Church of England to the science of the devout. Within these limits it is only possible to deal with three notable men.

Lancelot Andrewes (1555–1626), Bishop of Winchester, although distinguished as ecclesiastic, statesman, administrator and intimate counsellor of three monarchs, was greatest in the realm of conviction, character and devotion. As Gardiner puts it, "Of all those whose piety was remarkable in that troubled age, there was none who could bear comparison for spotlessness and purity of character with the good and gentle Andrewes. Going in and out as he did amongst the frivolous and grasping courtiers who gathered round the King, he seemed to live in a peculiar atmosphere of holiness, which prevented him from seeing the true

nature of the evil times in which his lot had
fallen." Once more is vindicated the promise,
"he that dwelleth in the secret place of the Most
High shall abide under the shadow of the Almighty." The devotional legacy contained in his
Private Prayers vibrates with the awe, reverence
and delight of a great soul. Dean Church, in his
analysis of the high service which Andrewes
rendered to the theological re-statement of the
doctrine of the Church of England in those
critical times, says truly that this led him on to
"a theology which ended in adoration, self-
surrender, and blessing, and in the awe and joy
of welcoming the Presence of the Eternal Beauty,
the Eternal Sanctity, and the Eternal Love, the
Sacrifice and Reconciliation of the world." Like
St. Augustine, "he is one of those who have left
us their very secret selves, as they placed themselves in the presence of their God and Saviour."
In the *Private Prayers* we realise that we are
standing on holy ground. The manuscript, in
Latin and Greek, blotted with tears, tells us how
intense was the struggle for holiness in this
crowded life. Counsellor and statesman, the
records show him to be, but with a greater certitude
our hearts assure us, as we strive to pray with him,
that here is a true saint of God.

Jeremy Taylor's life (1613–67) was still more
troubled by the divisions of his generation. Three

times was he imprisoned by the Puritans, in 1654, 1655 and 1657–8. Although created bishop after the Restoration, his was a troubled episcopate, ended prematurely by death from fever. He lives by his devotional and not by his theological and ecclesiastical writings. He himself declared that "Theology is rather a divine life than a divine knowledge." We are not, therefore, surprised that his great characteristics should be the high ideals which he sets before his readers, and the vigour with which he urges incentives to virtue. He will live for all time as the writer of two of the noblest manuals for the spiritual life that have ever been penned, *Holy Living* and *Holy Dying*. As the following chapters will indicate, they constitute a mine of teaching for those who would learn how to pray and how to meditate.

Thomas Wilson's career (1663–1745) nearly covers the next century. Bishop of Sodor and Man, he resolutely refused higher preferment, and remained in that almost savage isle, a devoted shepherd of the sheep. In his *Sacra Privata* he has left us a record of a life lived consciously in the presence of the Eternal, that is worthy to be placed on the library shelf side by side with the writings of St. John and Augustine and Andrewes. The whole of his life is sanctified by prayer. He prepares himself for marriage by prayer and writes a prayer to be said with his wife every morning.

Of his income as a bishop, he says, "I find I have enough and to spare, so that for the future I dedicate four-fifths to pious uses." When committed to prison by a preposterous decision of the Tynwald Court, he records his imprisonment under the heading of "Merciful Visitations." In a pastoral letter from prison he urges his people to "Let no unworthy thoughts enter into your hearts, nor unbecoming words come out of your mouths, against those that have given us this trouble." When an appeal to the Crown has secured a reversal of the Manx judgment, he refuses the King's offer of the See of Exeter that he might recoup himself, and he resolutely remains amongst his poor people, a Bishop indeed.

The *Sacra Privata* are less elaborate than the Private Prayers of Andrewes. They are more often meditations than prayers, but they record an arduous life, lived day by day in the "secret place of the Most High." The whole lesson of this remarkable human document, from which we shall learn much, is summed up in this passage on one of the opening pages, "He that hath learned to pray as he ought, has got the secret of a holy life."

When Rome was taken in 1870, the epitaph of one of the prisoners of the Inquisition was found scratched by his own hands on his prison wall, "Blessed Jesus, they cannot cast me out of Thy true Church." This sentence applied equally to

Baxter, Owen and Howe in 1662, when they were
expelled from their livings and cures of souls

Richard Baxter to John Wesley. 1650-1791. by the tragic Act of Uniformity. These men also belonged to the band of pilgrims making for the city which hath foundation, as truly as were

Chaucer's pilgrims making for Canterbury. Of one
of their number, Baxter himself gives a few lines
of brief biography of which we may say *Ex uno
disce omnes*. It was of Thomas Gouge that
Baxter wrote just after his death: "It would make
a volume to recite at large the charity he used to
his poor parishioners at Sepulchre's (before he was
ejected and silenced for Nonconformity). His
conjunction with Alderman Ashurst and some
such others, in a weekly meeting, to take account
of the honest poor families in the city that were in
great want, he being the treasurer and visitor; his
voluntary catechising the Christ's Church boys
when he might not preach; the many thousand
Bibles printed in Welsh that he dispersed in
Wales: the "Practice of Piety," "The Whole Duty
of Man," my "Call," and many thousands of his
own writing, given freely all over Wales; his setting
up about three hundred or four hundred schools in
Wales to teach children only to read, and the
Catechism; his industry to beg money for all this,
besides most of his own estate laid out on it; his
travels over Wales once or twice a year to visit his

schools and see to the execution; this was true
episcopacy of a silenced minister (who yet went
constantly to the parish churches, and was author-
ised by an old university licence to preach
occasionally, and yet for so doing was excom-
municate, even in Wales while he was doing all
this good). He served God thus to a healthful age
(seventy-four or seventy-six). I never saw him
sad, but always cheerful. About a fortnight
before he died he told me that some time in the
night some small trouble came to his heart; he
knew not what. And without sickness, or pain,
or fear of death, they heard him in his sleep give a
groan, and he was dead. O how holy and blessed
a life, and how easy a death!"

Of Richard Baxter, Lord Morley wrote that he
was "the profoundest theologian of them all"; and
S. R. Gardiner, the historian, says that he was
"the most learned and moderate of the Dissenters."
A considerable philosopher, he was one of the most
distinguished men of his day in many spheres, and
such was his devotion that Coleridge, in his
Notes on English Divines, says, "I could almost
as soon doubt the Gospel verity as his veracity.
Under . . . accursed persecutions he feels and
reasons more like an angel than a man." In an age
when intolerance was regarded as a virtue he could
write, insisting on the possibility of Papists "being
saved," and said, pleasing neither side, "We say

that a Papist as a Christian may be saved, but
not as a Papist." He adds this double-edged
illustration "as a man that hath the plague may
live, but not by the plague." The man who
preached his funeral sermon said, "In him the
virtues of the contemplative and active life were
united. His deportment was becoming a stranger
upon earth and a citizen of heaven." In his
famous work, *The Saints' Everlasting Rest*, he
writes with great sorrow of the contentions of
Christendom, and looking forward to that final
release he adds, "We shall then rest also from our
own sad divisions and unchristianlike quarrels
with one another." He sympathised neither with
the prelatists nor with the sectaries in their bitter
attacks upon each other, and he wrote, "the Lord
knows that, though my words may be too rough
and earnest, yet my soul longeth after the unity
and peace of the Church." His passion for unity
comes out in his *Apology for the Nonconformist
Ministry*, in which he says, "My time of service
is near an end; but *England* will be *England*, and
souls and the Church's peace will be precious, and
the cause will be the same when all present Noncon-
formists are dead: and bishops must die as well
as we." With a wide charity which strikes a note
that we should hardly have thought possible
in that century he writes, "Christianity is our
religion. Protesting against Popery is our

negation. . . . We still profess before men and
angels that we own no religion but the Christian
religion, nor any church but the Christian Church,
nor dream of any Catholic Church but one, con-
taining all the true Christians in the world, united
in Jesus Christ as the head. . . . Join not with
those men that cast out any ordinance of God
because the Papists have abused it. Reformation
of corrupted institutions is not by the abolition of
them, but by the restoration of them. There are
few things in use among the Papists themselves
as parts of worship but may lead us up to a good
original, or tell us of some real duty which did
degenerate into these.''

Baxter had a great joy in the assembly of the
saints. This comes out in his hymn, which begins:

"He wants not friends who hath Thy love
And may converse and walk with Thee,
And with Thy saints, here and above
With whom forever I must be."

He is revealed in these lines as a true citizen of
heaven.

In that last cruel trial by Jeffreys, who dis-
graced the name of Lord Chief Justice of England,
Baxter appeals with confidence to his own "life
and conversation known to many in this nation,"
and sums up his own confidence by saying, "these
things will surely be understood one day." None

can read his autobiography or his great devotional
works without realising that here is another
volume which may worthily be placed alongside
the *Confessions* of Augustine and the Prayers of
Andrewes and Wilson.

The apostolate of John and Charles Wesley,
which was so mightily to effect the character of
the English nation, and by its marvellous influence
on the manual workers of Great Britain, to make
possible in this twentieth century a Socialist
Government, led by a Presbyterian Prime Minister,
a Methodist Foreign Secretary, and a Chancellor
of the Exchequer trained in Methodism, began in
the Holy Club at Oxford. Overwhelming as was
the influence of his Evangelical conversion in 1738
upon the career of John Wesley, and a like
experience upon the life of his brother Charles, it
is true, as Nehemiah Curnock, the editor of his
Diary, has pointed out, that this Diary shows "that
for fifty-six years the club rules of Holy Living
formed the sub stratum of Wesley's daily devotion
and life." He himself wrote in one of his later
letters to his brother Charles, when the fruits of the
Evangelical revival established Methodism upon
a firm foundation, "I often cry out *Vitae me
redde priori*: let me be again an Oxford Methodist."
The frequent communion of those Oxford days
was maintained in the last year of his life, when
in December, 1790, he communicated seven

times, in January, 1791, nine times; February
was the month of his final illness, and he died on
4th March. On 21st October, 1735, during his
voyage to America, he thus describes a typical
day after the ship had fairly started that important
journey, "We now began to be a little regular; our
common way of living was this: from four in the
morning till five each of us used for private prayer;
from five to seven we read the Bible together; at
seven we breakfasted; at eight were the public
prayers; from nine till twelve I commonly learnt
German, my brother wrote sermons; at twelve we
met to give an account to one another of what we
had done since our last meeting, and what we
designed to do before our next. About one we
dined. From dinner till four we spent with the
people partly in public reading, partly in reading
to those whom each of us had taken in charge.
At four were the evening prayers, when either the
second lesson was explained, or the children were
catechised. From five to six we again used private
prayer; from six to seven I read in our cabin to
two or three of the passengers; at seven I joined
with the Germans in their public service; at eight
we met again to exhort and instruct one another;
between nine and ten we went to bed, where
neither the roaring of the sea nor the motion of the
ship could take away the refreshing sleep which
God gave us." Amongst all "who go down to the

sea in ships" was ever such a disciplined life recorded?

Fifty years later, on 23rd February, 1791, he wrote in his *Secret Diary* for the last time, and this was his record of how he lived within a week of Eternity: "4.45, prayed on business; read. 6.30, prayed. 7.0, read *Gustavus Vaga* [Vaga was a slave to whose writings Wesley refers in his letter to William Wilberforce, the last letter he ever wrote]. 9.0, with James Rogers. 10.30, at Mr. Belson's 1.2 Isaiah lv. 6. 2.0, dinner. 4.30, at Mr. T. F. . . . tea; conversed. 6.0, within. 8.0, supper; conversed. 9.30, prayed."

This day's experience was fairly typical of all. We know that whenever he conversed with anybody in those days it was to help them in the spiritual life. The secret of that apostolate was his Evangelical conversion, with this definite and steadily maintained background of a life of discipline and devotion. His *Secret Diary*, even more than his famous *Journal*, reveals a stern asceticism, a constant "buffeting of the body," as St. Paul terms it, in a life dependent upon unbroken fellowship with his Lord, quickened, as he tells us when preaching on the Eucharist, as the end of his ministry draws near, by what he calls "constant Communion." Such was the secret of that life which made possible and true the following passage with which Mr. Arnold Lunn concludes the latest biography of this greatest of English apostles and practical mystics: "The old world did not long survive John Wesley; it was 1791, and 'the rumble of a distant drum' had already proclaimed the blood-red dawn of revolution. England was to pass unscathed through those troubled years, but the tumbrils might well have been seen in the streets of London, had not a little man in gown and bands taken the world for his parish and changed the hearts of men."

The world has again been troubled by a bloody revolution, with its menace to the present civilisation; Wesley has given us the secret with which he held that such a danger could be averted. It is set out in one of his latest published letters, written to Alexander Mather on 6th August, 1777: "Give me one hundred preachers who fear nothing but sin and desire nothing but God, and I care not a straw whether they be clergymen or laymen, such alone will shake the gates of hell and set up the kingdom of heaven upon earth."

Chapter III

HOW TO PRAY

Charles Wesley, in one of those great love songs in which he expresses the passion of his heart for closer communion with Christ, asks to be shown

> "that happiest place,
> The place of Thy people's abode,
> Where saints in an ecstasy gaze
> And hang on a crucified God.
> 'T is there I would always abide
> And never a moment depart,
> Concealed in the cleft of Thy side,
> Eternally hid in Thy heart."

In these moments when the love of Jesus so possesses the soul, prayer is easy and, indeed, independent of vocal expression. But the ecstasies of a Wesley, a Francis, a Teresa, are exceptional, and ordinary disciples in every age will need the guidance which comes from the example of our Lord and of great souls who have left us the record of their inner life. In this chapter the endeavour will be made to hand on the lessons which they teach, and in so sacred a school to let the masters speak, and be oneself ever a learner.

It is important at the outset to emphasise the truth, which is accepted by all Christians, of the universal priesthood of believers.

The Universal Priesthood in Prayer Macaulay, in a somewhat rhetorical but eloquent passage, referred to the Puritans as looking down with contempt upon priests because "they esteemed themselves priests by the imposition of a mightier hand." But Macaulay's Puritan was not singular in his claim to share in a universal priesthood. Romanist and Anglican, Jesuit and Jansenist, theologians of all schools, recognise this great spiritual fact.

The Jesuit, Father Plus, says of the spiritual priesthood of which St. Peter speaks that it is an office so lofty that he does not hesitate to call it "a kingly priesthood. Some people do not like this title to be applied to the ordinary layman or woman, but there is no reason to be afraid of it— we should try and understand what it means. It is a grand word and expresses a great truth." The Oratorian, Saint Jean Eudes, with equal emphasis, says to his readers: "As you participate in the divine Priesthood of Jesus Christ, and as, in your character of Christian, and member of Jesus Christ, you possess the name and dignity of priest, you should exercise this dignity." We have therefore the support of Puritan, Jesuit and Oratorian, when we exercise our priesthood in prayer, and, in the words of the Prayer of Oblation in the Holy Communion, "offer and present unto Thee, O Lord, ourselves, our souls and bodies, to be a reasonable, holy, and lively sacrifice unto Thee."

The first necessity for effective prayer is, in Brother Lawrence's immortal phrase, "the prac-

**The Practice
of the
Presence**

tice of the presence of God," for the practice of that presence is the pathway to perfect love. Gratry, the great friend of Lacordaire, thus sums up this practice: "We must give up living in the outer and more superficial enclosure of the soul; we should go within and penetrate into its deepest recesses. And when we have arrived at this point, we must go still further in, until we reach the centre, which is no longer self, but God. There is the Master . . . and there it is that it may be vouchsafed us to abide with Him."

But some will say at once that such constant prayer as is here implied will conflict with daily duties. A mother absorbed in her thoughts of God will not, they imagine, be attentive to the needs of her children; she will fail in her simple home duties. This would be strangely to misunderstand what prayer demands. As George Herbert said long since:

> "Who sweeps a room as for Thy Laws,
> Makes that and the action fine."

We praise God best when we use His creatures as the means whereby He may be glorified. As Bossuet puts it, "continuous prayer does not consist in a perpetual tension of mind, but rather the keeping of ourselves in a state of dependence upon God, silently laying our needs before Him. Thus as the cracked parched earth by exposing her parched surface to the sky seems to be calling for rain, so the soul by exposing her wants to God appears to be saying: 'Lord, I have no need to pray to Thee; my needs, my state of indigence speak for me.' Thus we pray without words, and God understands this language."

St. Augustine expresses this thought simply, but with a certain note of irony, where he says: "If you are singing a hymn, you are praising God (always presupposing that you are thinking of the words). Then the hymn comes to an end, and it is time for a meal; if you keep yourself from overeating, you will be praising God. You go to your room to rest, and unless you get up with the set resolve to do something wrong, you will still be praising God. You go off to your business, and so long as there are no fraudulent dealings God will be praised. Are you a rural labourer?—then be sure that there are no weeds left in the ground you are digging, and once again this will be an occasion of praising God. Thus by the innocency of your works you will be praising God all the day long."

The whole of Brother Lawrence's work in the kitchen, to which he tells us he "had naturally a great aversion," was easy during the fifteen years that he was employed there, because, as he says, he had "accustomed himself to do everything there for the love of God, and with prayer upon all occasions." When he had to go into Burgundy to buy wine—a very unwelcome task for him, because he had no turn for business and because he was lame, and could not go about the boat but by rolling himself over the casks—he tells us "that he gave himself no uneasiness about it, nor about the purchase of the wine; that he said to God, 'It was His business he was about,' and that he afterwards found it very well performed."

The letters and conversations in which he describes his practice of the presence of God are included in the little volume *Retreats for the Soul*, and should be read by all who seek a more intimate fellowship with the Master. It is the triumphant record of a life of active service which was, nevertheless, "hid with Christ in God."

Saint Teresa, another great authority on the practice of the Presence, in the following passage from Chapter 30 of *The Way of Perfection* says: "It is of great profit for anyone to know that it is not necessary for him to raise himself to heaven

in order to converse with his divine Father and
find his happiness with Him, nor to elevate his
voice so as to be heard; God is so near that He
hears the slightest whisper from our lips and the
most secret thought. We have no need of wings to
go in search of Him; let us enter into the solitude
and look within us, it is there that He is. Let
us talk with Him in great humility, but also with
love, like children talking with their father,
confidently telling Him our troubles and begging
Him to help us, and recognising, above all, that we
are not worthy to bear the name of His children.
. . . For myself I own that I never knew what it
was to pray with satisfaction until He Himself
vouchsafed to teach me this salutary method. Let
him who desires to acquire this habit of the presence
of God, never weary of working little by little to
gain the mastery over himself, by recalling his
senses within himself. Far from losing, he will
find therein a great gain for his soul, that of re-
trenching the exterior use of the senses and of
making them subservient to his interior recollection." In another passage she writes: "For
years I was going through the trial of being unable
to fix my thoughts . . . it was extremely painful.
But I knew that our Lord condescends to keep
us company when we go to Him humbly and ask
Him for it. If a year passes without our getting
there, very well then! let it be several years. I

assure you that we can reach it, and we can with effort acquire the habit of living thus in the company of the greatest of all Masters."

Dr. Fosdick gives the teaching of others in a striking passage where he says: "Let any of the spiritual seers describe the innermost meaning of prayer to them, and always this habitual attitude of secret communion lies at the heart of the matter: they are seeking God Himself, rather than His outward gifts. As Horace Bushnell says: 'I fell into the habit of talking with God on every occasion. I talk myself asleep at night, and open the morning talking with Him'; and Jeremy Taylor describes his praying as 'making frequent colloquies and short discoursings between God and his own soul'; and Sir Thomas Browne, the famous physician, says: 'I have resolved to pray more and to pray always, to pray in all places where quietness inviteth, in the house, on the highway, and on the street; and to know no street or passage in this city that may not witness that I have not forgotten God.'"

It will help us in realising the presence of God to meditate upon the teaching of the Psalmist in Psalm 139 as to God's presence: "Thou compassest my path and my lying down, and art acquainted with all my ways. Whither shall I go from Thy spirit? or whither shall I flee from Thy presence? If I ascend up into heaven, Thou art there; if I make my bed in hell, behold, Thou art there. If I take the wings of the morning, and dwell in the uttermost parts of the sea; even there shall Thy hand lead me, and Thy right hand shall hold me."

Since we now know ourselves to be in the Presence of the King of Kings, let us act worthily

The Elements of Prayer

of our opportunity and consider —as we would if we had entered the presence of an earthly monarch from whom we hoped much—how we will address Him and what we will ask. Jesus has said that He will "give good things to them that ask Him," and

> "His grace and power are such
> None can ever ask too much."

But prayer is something vastly greater than mere petition. Even in the earliest prayer of childhood, when we asked that God would bless us, we added the petition that He would "make us good." In prayer we give God an opportunity "to do what His wisdom and love want done." As Dr. Fosdick reminds us, Eckhart has boldly said: "God can do as little without us as we without Him." George Eliot puts this in startling phrase when she says:

> "He will not make Antonio Stradivari's violins
> Without Antonio."

We do well to heed Savonarola's warning, "lest we be so busy talking to God that we cannot hearken to Him." If our prayer is to achieve its highest ends it must include many elements, and their enumeration, as emphasised by many masters of the spiritual life may help us now. These elements are (1) Adoration; (2) Confession; (3) Petition; (4) Intercession; (5) Thanksgiving; (6) Consecration.

Petition, therefore, is "only one province in the vast kingdom of prayer," and our instinct tells us that we must begin our prayer with **Adoration** Adoration. As we realise into Whose presence we have come, Adoration becomes inevitable. All of us easily recall occasions when we have spoken with some man or woman far greater than ourselves in position, character or achievement. We remember how nervous and anxious we were. We did not rudely rush into the presence of the great one as might some untutored fool. These reasons for reverence and adoration become supreme in our approach to our Father in Heaven. As our Lord Jesus Christ has taught us, our first thought should be of the Hallowing of His name. We may well ask that our prayer may be directed always to His Glory; that in His presence we should have no thought of anything but Him. We should consider with the eye of faith the infinite Majesty of God Who fills all things, in Whom we are "more immersed than the fish in the sea."

I adore Thee, Eternal Father, of Whom every fatherhood in heaven and earth is named, for the revelation of Thy Love in the gift of Thy Son for us men and for our salvation.

I adore Thee, Eternal Son, because Thou didst lay aside the glory of the Only Begotten and wast Incarnate by the Holy Ghost of the Virgin Mary for us men and for our salvation.

I adore Thee, Eternal Spirit, "Who dost Thy sevenfold gifts impart" for us men and for our salvation.

I adore Thee, gentle Jesus, born in Bethlehem and cradled in the manger for us men and for our salvation.

I adore Thee, My Saviour, tempted in the wilderness in all points like as we are and yet without sin, and therefore able to succour those who are tempted. I adore Thee who thus wast tried for us men and for our salvation.

I adore Thee, my Lord, enduring all the agony of Gethsemane for us men and for our salvation.

I adore Thee, O Crucified Saviour, suffering all the shame and anguish of the Cross for us men and for our salvation.

I adore Thee, my Risen and Triumphant Lord, because that Thou hast conquered death and the grave and hast opened up Eternal Life for us men and for our salvation.

I adore Thee, my Ascended Lord, that Thou hast not left us comfortless, but hast given to us Thy Holy Spirit to guide us continually in the pathway of salvation.

I adore Thee, O Holy Spirit, coming from the Father and the Son to give life and light and to preserve us from all the perils of this life and bring us to eternal salvation.

I adore Thee, O Holy, Blessed and Glorious Trinity, for giving to us the Grace of Our Lord, the Love of God, and the Fellowship of the Holy Ghost, and pray that in these we may for ever abide.

It is natural and inevitable that the thought of the holiness of the Eternal, of Whose Presence we are **Confession and Penitence** conscious, should waken, strengthen and confirm our sense of our own sinfulness and drive us to confession and penitence. Moses cried out: "Lord, Thou hast been our dwelling place in all generations. Before the mountains were brought forth or ever Thou hast formed the earth and the world, even from everlasting to everlasting, Thou art God,"; and it is this revelation of God which evokes the cry, "Thou hast set our iniquities before Thee, our secret sins in the light of Thy countenance."

In the solitude of the desert—which is always God's
antechamber—in the fierce light of the burning
bush, God's call to high service brings from Moses
the prompt reply, "Who am I that I should come?"

As we adore our Lord in His sinless body we
realise how black are our sins. Those tear-stained
pages on which Bishop Andrewes records his
prayers, open for us the door of the secret chamber,
and his words express our penitence as we pass
from adoration to confession and say with him:

"O Lover of men,
    very tenderly pitiful,
Father of mercies,
rich in mercy toward all that call upon Thee:
I have sinned against heaven and before Thee,
    neither am I worthy to be called a son,
    neither am I worthy to be made an hired servant,
        no, not the lowest of them all.
But I repent, alas, I repent:
help Thou mine impenitence:
be merciful to me a sinner.
Deep calleth unto deep,
the deep of our misery unto the deep of thy mercy.
Where sin abounded let grace much more abound:
overcome our evil with thy good:
let thy mercy rejoice against thy justice in our sins:
Thou that takest away the sins of the world,
    take away my sins:
Thou that didst come to redeem that which was
    lost, suffer not that to be lost which hath been
    redeemed of Thee.
I have deserved death:
    but even now I appeal from the seat of
    thy justice to the throne of thy grace."

So many regard prayer merely from the

standpoint of petition, or, at the best, think of

Petition and Intercession
prayer as petition for themselves and intercession for their friends, that it will be a surprise to some readers that this element should come so late in the consideration of the methods of prayer.   However, it is true, as Archbishop William Temple has said, that "prayer which is mainly occupied with a result to be obtained is comparatively powerless to obtain result."   It is supremely important for the efficacy of our petitions that we bring ourselves to a right attitude to God before we ask Him for those things that seem to us to be necessary, or desirable.   The Lord's promise of answers to prayer is based on the passage, "If ye abide in Me and My words abide in you, ye shall ask what ye will and it shall be done unto you."   On which Augustine comments: "For, abiding in Christ, how can they wish for anything but what befits Christ?"   Socrates, according to an ancient writer, "maintained that nothing further should be asked of the Immortals save that they should give us good things."   "Riches," said Socrates, "have been the destruction of many.   Honours have ruined many.   The possession of kingdoms has proved ill-fated, and splendid matrimonial alliances have ruined families."   Father Stanton expressed the truth very trenchantly when he said, "If God gave us all we asked for, I think most of

us would be in Hell by this time." Let us learn from Augustine, who tells us "It is lawful to pray for what it is lawful to desire." In one of his own petitions, recorded in the Confessions, he says: "O Lord my God, give me what Thou biddest, and then bid what Thou wilt." There is real force in the contention of Aquinas that we need to pray to God, not to make known to Him our needs or desires, but that "we ourselves may be reminded of the necessity of having recourse to God's help in these matters."

Sir Wilfrid Grenfell, speaking of the privilege of prayer as one of his most cherished possessions, said: "His answers I never venture to criticise. It is only my part to ask. It is entirely His to give or withhold as He knows best. If it were otherwise I would not dare to pray at all." I am reminded by these words of the fact that, as Dr. Fosdick points out, "Great disasters are due to answered prayers. Lot wanted Sodom and got it; Ahab craved the vineyard and siezed it; Judas desired the thirty pieces, and obtained them. They had their reward. The Bible is full of answered prayers that ruined men. As the Psalmist puts it, 'He gave them their request, but sent leanness into their soul.'" The story of Monica's prayer for her illustrious son, Augustine, is a great lesson that God gives us the substance of our desire, whilst He does not answer our petition. Monica prayed that God would not let her son sail for Italy, because she wanted Augustine to be a Christian and could not endure losing him from her influence. Whilst Monica prayed that Augustine might not sail, he left for Italy, came under the influence of Ambrose, and was converted in the very place from which his mother's prayers would have kept him. Augustine himself puts it thus: "Thou in the depth of Thy counsel, hearing the main point of her desire, regardedst not what she then *asked*, but that Thou mightest make me what she *ever desired*."

When John Huss was sentenced to death on June 8th, 1415, by the Council of Constance, one of his judges when his doom was read, asked him if he had aught to say. Answering never a word, he fell on his knees, "I pray to Thee God Almighty, I pray for everlasting life through Jesus Christ," That prayer comes under the terms of the promise "If ye shall ask anything in My name, I will do it."

Dr. Fosdick tells an interesting story from the Rabbis of a mother who had two sons, one a gardener and the other a potter. The gardener said, "O mother, pray God for rain to water my plants." The potter asked, "O mother, pray God for sunshine to dry my pots." The mother loved both equally well. Was it her duty to pray for rain or sun? Was it not best to leave it in the hands of God? In any case, the prayer of intercession for sinners cannot be contrary to the will of Our Lord. Bonaventura tells us of Francis of Assisi, that when he saw souls, redeemed with the precious blood of Jesus Christ, polluted by any stain of sin, he wept over them with such tenderness of compassion, that it seemed as though, motherlike, he was bringing them every day to birth in Christ. The heavenly vision that came to Saul of Tarsus on the road to Damascus was a threefold vision, a vision of Christ the Crucified, a vision of himself, and a vision of the world needing a Saviour. This vision will impel us to pray for the salvation of others, and this will always be in harmony with the will of the Redeemer.

Dr. John R. Mott, in an address on "Intercessors: The Primary Need," criticises with wonder the fact that there are not more and better intercessors. This wonder is caused by what we know of the character of God as revealed in Christ and the countless lessons that come from the experience of those who have given themselves to intercessory prayer, and the further fact that God's mightiest works are manifested only in the pathway of unselfish and persevering intercession. Dr. Mott expresses his conviction that "Two hundred men, yes, one hundred men of pure heart, unselfish motives, and unwavering faith in the integrity, omnipotence, love and present working of the living God, could, through intercession, usher in an era like unto that vital age, the age of Apostolic Christianity." It is surprising that there is so little intercession in the Christian Church to-day in view of our Lord's unequivocal teaching about prayer and His obvious wish that His followers should intercede; and the fact that He, whilst on earth, was an intercessor and still lives to make intercession for us.

Dr. Mott attributes the fact that there are not more intercessors to a lack of meditation upon God and His ways of working. If we study Christ and seek to imitate Him, we shall be led to intercession. In this practice he has found one of the great aids to faith. The other aid to faith that he places on an equality with the practice of intercession is the simple reflection that Jesus Christ prayed for others.

On these grounds Dr. Mott advises those whom he would teach to have a stated and unhurried time for intercession. One of the chief reasons, he believes, why Christ went apart for prolonged prayer was the fact that He had so much to do and that the issues of His life were so great. Therefore, he urges that none should wait for a leisured time for unhurried retreats with God on behalf of men. If ever that time comes, occasions which now demand our intercession will have passed by. Let us learn, he says, "to utilise unrecognised opportunities for intercession—on street cars, holding to the swaying strap, waiting at the station for trains, or in outer offices for appointments and interviews; before the beginning of a religious service, or during addresses, sermons and debates: on all these occasions to 'buy up the opportunity.'"

One thought of Dr. Mott's should give great comfort to those who are confined by sickness or other cause to their own room. One of his associates was laid aside by a serious illness for some years, and, on his bed of pain, in the long period of convalescence, siezed this the greatest opportunity of intercession that can come to a man. In Dr. Mott's opinion he has done more perhaps than any other member to make possible the releasing of the power of God in the Student Christian Movement.

It is right to interpolate a sentence at this point, and recognise the fact that there are certain orders in the Church of Rome, whose whole lives are devoted to intercession.

In concluding this admirable paper on intercession, Dr. Mott insists that, above all, we should realise the transcendent importance of increasing the number of men who will seek to release the power of God by prayer. He tells us that D. L. Moody used to say "A man is what he is in the dark." We may test the strength, the purity of our desire and motive by what we do where God alone sees us. He asks the question: "Are men moved to pray as the result of conscious or unconscious touch with our lives?" It is by the answer we are able to make to that question that we may test and measure the quality and influence of our own personal characters.

The world is full of lepers who have been healed and who have straightway forgotten the Great

Thanksgiving and Consecration

Physician. As Father Faber says: "Our own interests drive us obviously to prayer, but it is love alone which leads to thanksgiving. There is little enough of prayer, but there is still less of thanksgiving. And yet there is no redeemed soul that cannot echo the Psalmist's words, 'O that men would praise the Lord for His goodness and for His wonderful works to the children of men.' 'O give thanks unto the Lord, for He is gracious and His mercy endureth for ever.' "

When we consider the long list of mercies which we have received through no merit of our own, we must make a part of our worship the prayer: "O Lord God, what shall I render to Thy Divine Majesty for all the benefits Thou hast done unto Thy servant?" It is well that frequently we should recite in the silence of our time of communion with God the blessings that we have received at His hands, since we left our mother's knee. He has been our hope from our youth. He has saved us from temporal and spiritual danger.

And each one can recite the list of these deliverances, for which his gratitude must be forthcoming. There are special spiritual mercies which have been granted to us, for which our thanksgiving and our consecration are the least return that we can make. There are special times when such thanksgiving should characterise our prayers. Samuel Johnson, on his birthday every year, recognised the claims on him of the Divine Love, and prayed that "I may use Thy bounties according to Thy Will, through Jesus Christ Our Lord." John Wesley made these anniversaries also the occasion of special thanksgiving. We do well to have days when we say to ourselves, "I will remember the years of the Right Hand of the Most High."

The conclusion of our prayer must ever be an act of consecration. When we think of the infinite and innumerable mercies of God, we must be led to say with Fénelon: "I adore all Thy purposes without knowing them. I am silent. I offer myself in sacrifice. I give myself to Thee. I would have no other desire than to accomplish Thy Will." Before we return to the work of our daily lives, let us say with Augustine: "Let my soul take refuge from the crowding turmoil of worldly thoughts beneath the shadow of Thy Wing; let my heart, this sea of restless waves, find peace in Thee." Let us go forth to the battle of life, as Sir Jacob Astley went, before the Battle of Edgehill, when he said: "O Lord, Thou knowest how busy I must be this day. If I forget Thee, do not Thou forget me."

You must not rest short of a full and complete consecration. As we hear Our Lord saying: "Be ye, therefore, perfect," and St. Paul telling us that we are "called to be saints," we must remember, as it has been well said, that "Perfection is not a fixed and well defined goal to which we must attain under pain of having lost our way, but an endless road along which we continue to advance." As each day we seek to consecrate ourselves afresh, let us remember that "there is no progress but in the following of Christ." "If any man will come after Me, let him take up his Cross daily and follow Me." It is so easy to profess consecration to the Divine Purpose, and so hard to complete it. As Santa Teresa says, with gentle irony, "We think we are giving all to God, but in reality we are offering only the rent or produce, whilst we retain the fee simple of the land in our possession—a pleasant way this of seeking the love of God!" Finally, let us remember the promise for those who hunger and thirst after righteousness: "They shall be filled." God's free gifts are proportioned to our desire. Aquinas tells us that "prayer is the interpreter of a desire." Augustine reminds us that "we pray always by continually desiring in faith, hope and love." It is one of the splendid paradoxes of the

Christian life that to the heart desiring God there comes the response: "Thou wouldst not have sought Me hadst thou not already found Me." In times when faith falters, let us remember that great truth, and reconsecrate ourselves to God.

Some may say as they read this chapter, that prayer thus studied is complex and difficult. In its most elemental form prayer is as simple as breathing. On the other hand, as Coleridge has said, "of all mental exercises, earnest prayer is the most severe." If the task be arduous, the reward is great. This is summed up effectively in a passage which San Pedro of Alcantara, the great Franciscan teacher of the devout life, quotes from Bonaventura:

"If you would endure with patience the adversities and miseries of this life,
  Be a man of prayer.
If you would acquire strength and courage to vanquish the temptations of the enemy,
  Be a man of prayer.
If you would know the wiles of Satan and defend yourself against his snares,
  Be a man of prayer.
If you would live with a gay heart, and pass lightly along the road of penance and sacrifice,
  Be a man of prayer.

If you would drive away vain thoughts and
   cares which worry the soul like flies,
Be a man of prayer.
If you would nourish the soul with the sap of
   devotion and have it always filled with good
   thoughts and desires,
Be a man of prayer.
Finally, if you would uproot from your soul
   all vices, and plant virtues in their place,
Be a man of prayer,
For herein does a man receive the unction and
   grace of the Holy Spirit, who teaches all
   things."

From another writer, San Pedro quotes the
following passage with which this chapter may
fitly end: "Great are the excellences of prayer,
great its privileges. The heavens open before it,
and unveil therein their secrets, and to it are the
ears of God ever attentive."

Chapter IV

THE ART OF MEDITATION

THE first question that confronts us as we seek to enter into the full privileges of friendship with Jesus, is to ask how meditation differs from those elements of prayer which we have considered in our last chapter. It is not enough for us to say that one is vocal and the other is silent. The masters of the spiritual life from the psalmists and the prophets down the ages to the saints of each succeeding generation of the Church's history have found in meditation an approach to the footstool of the Divine mercy and love which because of its very intimacy has been beyond the power of expression. In the human relationships of child to parent, of parent to child, of husband to wife, we have often experienced the impossibility of expressing our deepest devotion in words. As someone has said, "a point is reached when the exchange of gifts is not called for, because the gift of the heart is known to be mutually and eternally complete." We can never complete our surrender to our Lord until the opportunities of loving service on earth are ended, but as the sense of His friendship and love grow stronger, as the thought of all His gifts is deepened, we shall know that it would need "a thousand tongues to sing our great Redeemer's praise."

It is important in considering the different methods for perfecting the Art of Meditation that emphasis should be laid on the fact that all methods are means to an end. Those who find them useless will be well advised to leave stereotyped methods, and follow those the helpfulness of which is proved by experience. As Ludovic de Besse points out, "books are ladders of ascent which in time should be discarded. Those who are engaged in the active affairs of the world should especially use the greatest liberty in the choice of time, place, and other means. The rule should be for each to choose the means which succeed best with him, even though others find them unsuitable." Santa Teresa advises us that we should "make use of meditation to place ourselves in the company of our Lord, and reflect on Him in the state corresponding to our own feelings at the time. When full of joy, meditate on His Resurrection; if sorrowful, join Him in the Garden of Olives, always remembering that the time given to meditation is the occasion when the heart speaks to God, and, what is of infinitely greater moment, when God speaks to the heart."

There is, as has already been implied, a true apostolic succession in the line of those who have taught most concerning meditation from St. Paul and St. John to Augustine and his successors. The *Confessions* of Saint Augustine, dating from the end of the fourth century, are one long series of meditations. This book provides, for all who wish to learn how to meditate, the most valuable guide outside the apostolic writings. Seven centuries later, Bernard of Clairvaux gives us the first rule for successful meditation. "Leave there at the door all thy business matters, and resume them again on thy departure. But thou, my soul, enter alone into the sanctuary of the Lord in order to abandon thyself entirely to His love."

In our meditation we do well to be aware of the danger of a harmful self-contemplation made under the pretext of the examination of conscience. As Bossuet says: "There is a very great difference between holy reflections which inspire us with the love of God, and the ceaseless return upon ourselves which is the source of self-love." But, as Tauler writes, "where God Himself dwelleth in the man, . . . where there is this union, which is the offspring of Divine light and dwelleth in its beams, there is no spiritual pride or irreverent spirit, but boundless humility, and a lowly broken heart."

The Brothers of the Common Life, the German mystics of the fourteenth century, Eckhardt,

Tauler, Suso, and Ruysbroek, made a great "effort to maintain the spirit of ordered personal religion and communion with God, in the face of growing insistence upon bare obedience to the hierarchy in externals." This disciplined life had its home in Holland. Gerhard Groot, a professor from Cologne, gathered round him at Deventer a young group of students, whom Dr. Kirk in his Bampton Lectures called a "Methodist Community." They were known as "the Brothers of the Common Life." It was this community which met at Grindelwald in conference for the deepening of the spiritual life. They originated the general movement known as "the New Devotion," of which Thomas à Kempis, 1380–1471, was the most notable product.

The New Devotion passed onward to a name pregnant with great influence for good and evil in the history of the Church. One Gansfort, an eccentric friend of Thomas à Kempis, drew up a "Ladder of Meditation," which was used by Garcia de Cisneros, Abbot of Montserrat, in preparing his Spiritual Exercises, a book which was published in 1500. Twenty-two years later one of the monks of that monastery became confessor to a young Spanish pilgrim, Ignatius Loyola, who was to write at Manresa his "Exercises," the influence of which on Christendom it is difficult to overstate. They are infused with the spirit and aim of à Kempis's great work, and make their appeal for meditation on the Incarnate Lord "to bring the soul nearest to the contemplation of the Eternal Godhead."

It is difficult to determine what is the exact value that the ordinary Christian should attach to the methods of Ignatius, and what is their place in the development of the Art of Meditation. It is nearly forty years since the writer, when visiting Rome with the address of the Grindelwald Conference to Pope Leo XIII, was given a copy of the *Exercises* by Alfred Gatty, the brother of Mrs. Ewing. For a man in the full pressure of life, this work has not been found comparable in helpfulness with à Kempis's *Imitation of Christ* or *The Spiritual Combat* by Scupoli. There are many elements in the Ignatian training which would inevitably be criticised by those who will read these pages. At the same time there is something of much value for all. Ignatius propounds five methods of meditation. The first, on the Commandments, comprises Preparation, which consists of Self-examination, to ascertain how far the Commandments have been broken; Meditation and Prayer on the deadly sins and their contrary virtues, and on the powers of the soul; and a Colloquy with our Lord in familiar and intimate loving conversation.

The Ignatian Methods

The second method seems to be better adapted
to the case of the ordinary person. It is to take a
prayer, such as the Lord's Prayer, and dwell upon
the meaning of each word. It is astonishing how
many people repeat prayers without thought, and
the adoption of this method will bring home this
fact immediately to those who use it. The third
method consists in reciting vocal prayers with
care and devotion, and has some kinship with
the second method. The fourth method has least
to commend itself to-day. It recommends that
we shall think of the souls in Hell and thank
God that we have been saved from such
a fate.

The fifth is especially the Ignatian method. It
commences with a careful preparation made over-
night, the asking of ourselves a series of questions
beginning with the interrogatives, Who? What?
Where? By what aid? Why? How? When?
For whom? With what love? With what
truth? Ignatius recommends that not more than
three of these should be used on each occasion,
the main object being to concentrate on what
we desire to gain from our prayer. This thorough
preparation is followed by an elaborate system
of meditation which may well be called
" Exercises."

It is quite clear that such a system of
examination and meditation is only possible to

those who possess certain special aptitudes and much freedom from worldly affairs.

Baron von Hügel in his delightful work, *The Life of Prayer*, has an interesting comment on the complexity of this system of meditation. He says that "when Frederick William Faber preached the panegyric of St. Ignatius Loyola, on the occasion of the Feast of the Founder of the Jesuits, in the Jesuit church at Farm Street, he spent an hour in unbroken, sympathetic, indeed fervent, exposition of this saint's spirituality, and only in his last sentence did he introduce the necessary limitation and expansion: "This, then my dear brethren, is St. Ignatius's way to heaven; and, thank God, it is not the only way!"

No one can read the devotional literature of the centuries without realising the ever-increasing heritage of the Church of Christ **A Franciscan** that has been handed down by **Method** the great saints whose passionate devotion to our Lord makes them stand out "like peaks of some sunk continent jutting through oblivion's sea." The outstanding Franciscan teacher of the Art of Meditation is San Pedro of Alcantara (1499–1562) in a volume on *Prayer and Meditation*. This little book may well be the companion of any who wish for guidance in a "retreat." It contains a complete scheme of meditation, which in one act would

E

occupy approximately two hours. Father Bede Frost, commenting on this book, says: "In our restless and nerve-ridden day, this may seem excessive." Even Santa Teresa, when recommending that two hours be spent in mental prayer, said that for some years she "was more occupied with the wish to see the end of the time appointed and in watching the hour-glass than with other thoughts that were good." Nevertheless, San Pedro's little volume furnishes a guide of great value to the way in which meditation may each day guide our devotion to one dominating thought. St. Teresa said of him, "It is not surprising that one who practised it with so much purity, should have written on it so well and so profitably." St. Francis de Sales said: "Alcantara is very good for prayer." His volume of meditations provides for a meditation for every day in the week, also for seven meditations for Holy Week, and a remarkably complete outline of meditation for all occasions, which will be used as the basis for an outline of the method of meditation which will follow towards the end of this chapter.

We have already seen that, in her own comment on the hour-glass, Santa Teresa brings a certain sanity to bear upon the devout life. There is a quiet humour about the passages from her

The Teresian Teaching

writings dealing with this question that is of real
value, and something very beautiful about the
simplicity of some of her thoughts. "Picture
our Lord close beside you. See how lovingly,
how humbly He is teaching you. Practise it!
Practise it! I am not now asking you to meditate
upon Him, nor to produce great thoughts, nor to
feel deep devotion. I only ask you to look at
Him." Centuries later the Curé d'Ars repeated
that thought; he only just "looked" at the Lord
whom he loved.

Again, in another passage, Santa Teresa tells us
to place ourselves "in the presence of Christ and,
without *fatiguing the understanding*, converse with
Him, and rejoice in Him without wearying ourselves in searching out reasons."

There is one special thought that stands
out in the teaching of Santa Teresa: it is that
"we should ever meditate on the greatness and
majesty of our God," and that we should turn
away from the thought of ourselves and realise
that "we shall advance more by contemplating
the Divinity than by keeping our eyes fixed on
ourselves." This is most important for all who
would cultivate the habit of meditation. She
goes on to say: "I think we shall never learn
to know ourselves except by endeavouring to
know God, for beholding His greatness we are
struck by our own baseness. His purity shows

our foulness, and by meditating on His humility, we find how far we are from being humble." Again, "Always begin and finish your prayer with the thought of your own nothingness." In another passage: "His Majesty loves and seeks courageous souls, but they must be humble in their ways and have no confidence in themselves."

The vital contribution to the cultivation of the devout life made by St. Francis de Sales (1567–1622), the great Bishop of Geneva, **St. Francis de Sales** was for the first time addressed not to the cloister, but to those who were living in the full tide of an active everyday life. His great namesake, Francis of Assisi, had instituted the Third Order for the laity. But this was in itself an Order. Francis de Sales goes much further, and pleads for the "Devout Life" of the ordinary layman. In the third chapter of his *Introduction to the Devout Life*, he says that "It is an error, nay rather a heresy, to wish to banish the devout life from the army, from the workshop, from the courts of princes, from the households of married folk." He recognizes that the monastic and religious type of devotion cannot be practised in these surroundings, and claims that there are other types of devotion which "are suitable for leading to perfection those whose lives are spent in secular avocations." He appeals to the example of the great names both in the Old and New

Testaments, and notable characters in the history
of the Church, like St. Monica in her household,
Cornelius in the army, St. Louis and St. Edward
on their thrones, in support of his contention. He
even reminds a lady in the full tide of court life to
whom he is writing, to remember that many have
lost perfection in solitude, notwithstanding that it
is so favorable to perfection, and have preserved it
amidst the multitude, which seems so little favorable to perfection. Wherever we are, he urges that
we may, and we ought to, aspire to the perfect life.

Literature was enriched in the XVIIth
Century by the writings of two bishops on

XVIIth Century. Anglican and Puritan

this subject, which Wesley included in that remarkable col-
lection published in thirty
large octavo volumes, entitled
The Christian Library. Joseph Hall, Bishop of
Exeter, was first described by Thomas Fuller as
"Our English Seneca for the purenesse, plainnesse
and fullnesse of his style. Not unhappy at Controversy, more happy at Comment, very good in
his Character, better in his Fairness, best of all in
his Meditations." He laid down certain wise rules
and said: "In Meditation those who begin heavenly
thoughts and practise them not are like those that
kindle a fire under green wood and leave it as soon
as it begins to blaze. When I set myself to meditate
I will not give over until I come to an issue. It has

been said by some that the beginning is as much as
the middle; yea more: but I say, the ending is more
than the beginning. When the mouth prayeth,
man heareth; when the heart, God heareth.''

Simon Patrick, Bishop of Ely, is the other
bishop of the Church of England whose meditations find a place in this library. They are
especially a series of meditations on "The Christian
Sacrifice," and set out the "Necessity, End and
Manner" of receiving the Holy Communion.

It is, however, in the writings of Richard Baxter
the Puritan, that Wesley finds teaching on
Meditation, and especially in the well-known work
The Saints' Everlasting Rest which he includes
in its entirety in the Christian Library. Baxter
declares that meditation is a duty of God's ordain-
ing, but that it is a duty constantly practised he
with sorrow must deny. "Whilst men," he says,
"are troubled if they miss a sermon, a psalm, or a
prayer in public or in private, yet they are never
troubled that they have omitted meditation perhaps
all their lifetime to this very day." He goes on to
say that as a man spends half an hour taking into
his stomach that meat which he must have seven
or eight hours to digest, so a man may take into
his understanding and memory more truth in one
hour than he is able well to digest in many. It is
clear that Richard Baxter was acquainted with
many of the writings which have already

contributed to this chapter. He realises with Santa
Teresa that the first essential for those who "set
out on this work" is that they should "labour to
have the deepest apprehension of the presence of
God and of the incomparable greatness of the
majesty which they approach." If his reader con-
siders "the blessed issue of the work and if it
succeed it would be an admission indeed into the
presence of God, the beginning of thy eternal glory
on earth, a means to make thee live above the
rate of other men and admit thee into the next
room to the angels themselves, a means to make
thee live and die both joyfully and blessedly, so that
the prize being so great thy preparation shall be
answerable."

What Baxter called the chief part of the business
of meditation he held to be the reading over of the
promises, studying all confirming providences,
pouring forth our own experiences, and remembering the Scriptures already fulfilled both in the
Church and State in the former ages, and eminently
both in the present age and those that are being
fulfilled particularly to-day. He writes, "Thus do
thou expatiate in the praises of God and open His
excellency to thine own heart, till thou feel the life
beginning to stir and the fire in thy breast beginning
to kindle." He bids us remember the word of
Augustine, "The soul that loves ascends frequently
and runs familiarly through the streets of the

heavenly Jerusalem, visiting the patriarchs and prophets, saluting the apostles, and admiring the armies of martyrs and confessors. So," he says, "do thou lead on thy heart as completely free, bringing it into the palace of the great King; lead it as it were from chamber to chamber; say to it, 'Here must I lodge, here must I live, here must I love and be beloved.'" It is interesting to find him warning his reader against the use of pictures as practised by "the Papists," but he proceeds, with many of the Roman writers, to urge us to get "the liveliest picture of these things in thy mind that possibly thou canst. Meditate on them as if thou wert all the while beholding them, and as if thou wert even hearing the Hallelujahs, until thou canst say 'Methinks I see a glimpse of the glory; methinks I hear the shouts of joy and praise; methinks I even stand by David and Peter and Paul and more of these triumphing souls; methinks I see the Son of God appearing in the clouds, and the world standing at His bar ro receive their doom; methinks I hear Him say "Come ye blessed of my Father," and see them go rejoicing in the joy of their Lord.'"

He urges us in our meditation to compare the things we shall enjoy above with the excellency of those admirable works of providence which God does exercise in the Church and in the world. He also bids us compare the mercies that we shall have above with the particular providences enjoyed here; the joy which we shall have in heaven with that which the saints of God have found in the way to it.

His plea for meditation concludes with this powerful passage: "But for you whose heart God has weaned from all things here below, I hope you will take one walk daily in the New Jerusalem! God is your love and your desire, and I know you would fain be more acquainted with your Saviour, as I know it is your grief that your hearts are not more near to Him; and that they do not more passionately love and delight in Him. As ever you would enjoy your desires, try this life of meditation on your everlasting rest."

The Evangelical Revival which began with the "Holy Club" at Oxford two hundred years ago, and the Anglo-Catholic Revival of a century later, each of them emphasised the value of meditation. The followers of John Wesley, "Homo Unius Libri," have found in the sacred writings, and also in Wesley's hymns, the subjects for, and the training in meditation that gave depth and strength to the Revival. For millions of Methodists the Bible and Wesley's hymns have been, in earlier generations, the whole of their devotional literature, and they have not suffered thereby. The Anglo-Catholics, Keble, Pusey and others, nevertheless, wisely directed their followers also to the writings of the Saints of

Listening

the Universal Church, and claimed their share in
the heritage of the ages, in the writings of Augustine, à Kempis, Scupoli, Francis de Sales, and
others. But it is important to add that Pusey and
Newman were as intensely biblical as Wesley and
Spurgeon.

And now for the third time in its history Oxford
is claiming the attention of the religious world. A
little band of Oxford men, who include a distinguished Bampton Lecturer, now Oriel Professor
of the Christian religion, and Fellows of Hertford,
Corpus Christi and Lincoln College, Oxford, and
others who combine scholarship with such
distinctions in sport as would have startled Wesley
and Pusey: these men are avowing themselves
followers of Dr. Frank Buchman, an American
Lutheran Pastor. His teaching is marked by an
insistance on the claims of spiritual religion, with
a special emphasis on the importance of meditation
in what the Groups term "the Quiet Time." The
new emphasis in their message is expressed in
their phrase to "listen in" to God, and in their
constant use of the word "guidance," and their
confident belief that they are directed individually
and corporately, by the immediate inspiration of
the Holy Spirit. In some respects the movement
is a renaissance of Early Methodism, in other it is
closely akin to the message of George Fox and the
Quakers, and it is also affected by the teaching on

grace and the theology of crisis which characterise Barth and his school.

This reference to the Oxford Groups is interpolated just as this little book was passing through its final revision, and this is the result of intimate personal contact with some of the leaders during, and immediately after, the last Wesleyan Methodist Conference. There was something specially significant in the fact that through a series of apparent accidents, which these men attribute to the Direct Guidance of God, the writer met two of them on the eve of the first Sunday of the Conference, and hurriedly arranged for what became in effect one of their house parties. On this occasion the Rev. Geoffrey Allen, Chaplain and Fellow of Lincoln College, spoke to the gathering, which included the President of the last Wesleyan Methodist Conference, the successor of that first President of the Methodist Conference who replied to the Bishop, rebuking his unconventional methods, "as Fellow of Lincoln College, Oxford, I was ordained Priest of the Universal Church." There were others present who had also filled Wesley's Presidential chair, and held, each for one year, his seal of office and his "Field" bible. It may therefore, be of interest to quote from a letter received from Mr. Geoffrey Allen, after he had read the proof sheets of this chapter. He writes: "I should now personally be inclined to put very great emphasis on listening to God in prayer; or just resting quiet and hearing His voice speak through conscience, which is His instrument for speaking; and on letting Him take the initiative. I personally did not find the various mystical manuals of devotion very helpful, as a ladder of ascent to God; for me they helped to some extent to create a mood of devotion, but they did not lead me to the knowledge of Christ, as I have since been led. I found that I had to let God in full realism do most of the speaking, even if it meant listening to His opinion of spheres of life, of which I did not like to hear. I found I had to let Him in quiet point out where I had offended, and further lead me to the costly step of acknowledging to other men where I had offended. I found and find that where I do let God speak in this way, convicting me of sin, then in quiet He also speaks, guiding me to concrete actions which are in accordance with His will. Where sin has been faced before Christ and forgiven and acknowledged, there I find that the voice of God in conscience is heard more clearly, leading to other things. In practice too I find that to listen to God in this kind of way in prayer, and to obey even in quiet small things, very often opens the door to other larger spheres of service, into which otherwise I should not have been led.''

The importance of the time given to meditation depends wholly in their view on *The Fact of God's*

Guidance. As one of them put it to the writer, "The more work I have to do, the greater the pressure of my duties, the longer must I listen to God." That statement is taken so literally that the group sits, each one with paper and pencil, to note down God's messages. These are then compared and "checked."

They claim that experience shows that a converted life can be guided in all things by God's Holy Spirit working through the human mind. They are convinced, and they claim that it is on the basis of personal experience, that the only barrier that can prevent a man from hearing God and understanding His will is sin. They insist that on each one is laid the obligation of mediating to the world what they learn in active communion with God. At the same time, they contend that the conditions for guidance are absolute honesty, absolute purity, absolute unselfishness and absolute love. God must be sought for Himself. Self-discipline must be observed in keeping a regular, unhurried time for quiet waiting upon God.

They lay down a number of tests to prove that the guidance that comes is from God, and is not a delusion. To this end they exchange experiences and consider the message that each is convinced that he has received. Like George Fox and the early Quakers, they insist upon the value of "united quiet" and "corporate silence." There must be discipline, the regular observance of the morning watch, and a refusal to stop short of whatever is required to bring up the individual to his highest point, in body, mind, spirit and social relationship.

Whilst recognising that "the guided life calls for great human risks, much blazing of trails by faith," yet they hold that "life under God's hand" often calls us to act upon probabilities rather than upon certainties. These probabilities they would check by constant reference to the Bible, which, to use their language, "expresses the experience through centuries of men who have dared under Divine revelation to live experimentally with God." They ask that their guidance shall be checked by coincidence, and that the question that shall be asked at every point is "Where is the Cross?" For ultimately we are called to what is "essentially the fellowship of a Crusade." Whilst the result of this guidance will be "an intuitive conviction that the course of action is inherently right," we must ask "What others say to whom God speaks." This, they assert, is the "unwritten law of fellowship."

This survey of the place given to meditation in the experience of religious teachers from the birth **The Method of** of Christianity to the present **Meditation** time justifies the conclusion that no success in propagating their faith has ever been divorced from this practice by any of the great missionaries of the Faith. Therefore, we are driven to ask what will be our own individual methods. In considering this vital question we must not be discouraged by the difficulties of the task. Although an endeavour is now made to outline a method, it is well that we should each form our own plan.

"On with toil of heart and knees and hands," we
    seek to reach
"Those shining table-lands,
  To which our God Himself is moon and sun."

We are no holiday mountaineers travelling in our own time and way. We are following the

      "Leader of faithful souls, and Guide
        Of all that travel to the sky,"

and we must go by the narrow track that He points out, "o'er moor and fen, o'er crag and torrent." The pathway may seem to us a "mighty maze," but it is "not without a plan." It is a well-trodden way, and we would learn from all who have left their marks on the path to guide us in our mountain climb. The following method is, therefore, compiled from the directions of many great teachers.

I.   PREPARATION.

(a)   All teachers agree that we must seek to realise the presence of God. When Sir George White at Ladysmith commenced his daily private prayers he always stood at attention. That must be our attitude. "Speak, Lord, for Thy servant heareth." We are speaking to One who is truly present, and our conversation with Him is no vain imagination but a supreme reality.

(*b*) Humility is the only possible attitude in which we can commence our meditation. "The greatest of sinners can pray, provided only he prays as a sinner."

(*c*) We must ask for the grace of renunciation, that we may give up our own purposes and enter into union with our Lord and His desires.

(*d*) We must invoke the Holy Spirit that our meditation may have His assistance and help.

In our preparation it is essential that we should look away at once from ourselves and look to God. We shall gain more by meditating upon the Divine reality, by looking to our Lord on the Cross, than by considering the need of avoiding sin and fighting temptation, and of resisting evil. The passion of love for our Lord which marked the Revival of the eighteenth century was the positive power that conquered the degradation and sin of the sunken masses of that age. The expulsive power of the love of Jesus has driven out devils in all places and at all times when the more negative commands of Sinai failed to secure national righteousness. Our object in our meditation must be to ponder upon the majesty of God, the grace of our Lord Jesus Christ, and the gift of the Holy Spirit, and in so doing we shall get away from our own temptation and sin. We shall most effectively prepare ourselves for our meditation by an act of adoration of the Divine Majesty, by the realisation of our own failure to obey His commands, and by coming before Him in the name of Jesus, and invoking the Holy Spirit of Jesus to guide us in our meditation.

II. MEDITATION.

The subject of our meditation will vary from day to day, but the supreme object will be to show our affection towards our Lord and towards the Divine King. If one subject taken for meditation does not help us at the time, we are advised by the masters of meditation to pass on to another, "always gently and simply without undue haste."

We may choose many subjects for our meditation, but the end of all prayer and meditation is three-fold: to see Jesus, to be united with Jesus, to work in Him. Adoration is the first, Communion is the second, and Co-operation is the third.

The final object of our meditation comes under seven heads: The Christian (1) ought to adhere to Christ; (2) to put on Christ; (3) to abide in Christ; (4) to live with Christ; (5) to live the life

of Christ risen from the dead; (6) to go by the
spirit of Christ and to do all things in His Name and
Spirit; (7) to put on the character and virtues of
Christ living in Heaven.

III.   Conclusion.

When our meditation is ended we are called
upon:

(1)   To thank God for the privilege;

(2)   To place all our resolutions in our Lord's
hands, assured that He alone can help us to keep
them;

(3)   To offer all our affections and resolutions to
God in the name of His Son.

The last revision of these pages had gone to the
printer when a distinguished member of the
Advisory Committee wrote to

Vocal and Mental Prayer

ask what after all is the difference
between vocal and mental prayer.
The old peasant understands when kneeling before
the Cross.   He says in his simple fashion: "I just
looks at Him, and He looks at me."   The lovers
understand when no more gifts need to be exchanged because the gift of life is complete.   They
sit in silence rejoicing in the reality of their love
for each other with a joy that words cannot express.
Before the majesty and the might of the Eternal,
the soul prostrates itself in an adoration akin to,

but more profound than, that which overwhelms us when for the first time there bursts upon our vision the full glory of the sunset, the snowclad mountain top, or the equal glory on the plain of the clouds, and of the rainbow, when the sun bursts through the tempest. We may find the Fifty-first Psalm adequate—as so many millions have done—to express our penitence as we confess our sins, but when the confession is made, the blackness of our ingratitude contrasted with the infinite love of God makes even these words insufficient. When in our meditation we pass on to the needs of others, we realise how much our prayers gain in reality, if we replace verbal expression by thought on the needs of each soul for whom we pray. Prayers have failed, because the phrases of a lifetime have lost their vitality when there has been no deep and sustained thought as to their foundation in reality to keep them alive. And when we ponder on the message from God's Word from which we seek help, words only impede us, as they would in the solution of any of the greater problems of time and space. Thought is limited by verbal expression, and we call meditation in aid to give free and full expression to the deepest desires of the heart.

A warning must be given: Not to allow ourselves to be trammelled in our conversations with our Lord by any method that any of the teachers of the Church have devised. We must leave

ourselves free to follow the leading of the Holy
Spirit.

Let us ever remember that meditation upon
virtues without putting them into practice is vain
and dangerous.   As Butler said in his great
Analogy, "Passive impressions are weakened by
repetition and do not of themselves form habits."
Meditation that does not lead to active service will
not help us in the following of our Lord, and that is
the supreme end of all meditation.

The words of St. John of the Cross will fitly close
this chapter: "Let us run after God, for we may be
sure He will not fly from us.   He is nailed upon the
Cross, and infallibly we shall find Him there.   Let
us convey Him into our hearts, and then shut the
door that He retire not thence."

Chapter V

THE DISCIPLINE OF LOVE

"The supreme purpose of the world is discipline, and the supreme guide through its perplexities is duty."—JOHN OMAN.

THE discipline necessary to make us perfect soldiers of Jesus Christ in a world that is unceasingly fighting against Him, will find its inspiration and direction in Love, the master passion of life. This is the great need of the Church to-day. The poet must not mislead us when he says:

Love took up the harp of life and smote on all the
  chords with might,
Smote the chord of self that, trembling, passed in
  music out of sight.

A great passion may change life and character, but we err if we think that self vanishes either "in music" or otherwise at one stroke. The Master Potter does not mould the vessel to His will with one turn of the wheel. His Hand must shape and fashion it in many ways, but always with the love of the Supreme Artist, before the vessel can be perfected.

The contemplation of the Love of Jesus for us

The Discipline of the Love of Jesus for us
is the first call to a discipline of self which, if inward, shall not be less real than that of the soldier preparing for and going into the battle which means wounds and death to him.

The Lord of Love has been crucified, and is still every day being crucified afresh by the sins of those for the love of whom He was made man. The world bought by the agony and shame of the Cross rejects its redemption by Incarnate Love, listens to the song of hate and joins in the chorus. The wounded Heart is day by day torn open again by the spear point of some world tragedy of wrong. The Hands that always sought to bless, the Feet that ever went about doing good, are daily pierced anew by the malice and hate that reject the blessing and scorn the good, and again and again as the beloved knows the sorrows of the Divine Lover he cries, "My Lord, my Love, is crucified." The sun in its circuit of the world is always rising on new Calvaries, and thereby to each one of us comes the task "to fill up on (his) part that which is lacking in the sufferings of Christ for His Body's sake, which is the Church."

O Blessed Lord Jesus, Whose hands, once stretched out upon the Cross, now clasp us in the embrace of Infinite Love, compel us, we pray

*Thee, by our sense of the greatness of that Love,
to seek the conquest of everything in our hearts
and lives that is unworthy of Thee. May Thy
Love shame us out of all self-indulgence and help
us to suffer hardship with Thee as our Leader
and Captain. May all pride and vanity be
driven out of our lives by our knowledge of the Love
that humbled Itself to our low estate. Thy Love
has pursued us unceasingly amid all our selfishness
and selfwill, and has overtaken us in our wanderings. Let that Love still hold us fast, rejoicing
that we have been made captive to do Thy will,
here and hereafter, now and forever, through the
grace given by Thyself, our Lord and our Love.
Amen.*

The love which responds to Infinite Love, our
Love of Jesus, is unworthy of its object if it does
not suffice to compel us to all the disci-
The Disci- pline that is necessary to fit us for
pline of our His service. "We love Him because
Love for He first loved us." If that is the reason
Jesus of our love, the Cross must be the
measure of our love. Therefore it is that Jesus
speaks with such ruthless plainness to those who
follow Him. Their motives, like ours, are many.
He will be loved for Himself alone. They, with
high purpose, seek a Kingdom of Righteousness in
which they would be His chief Ministers. He

replies to their longings with a sharpness that
teaches them once for all the measure of their
ambition. "Can ye drink of the cup that I drink
of?" He seeks their sympathy and tells them
of the discipline that He must undergo. "Though
He was a Son, yet learned He obedience through
the things that He suffered." But as He speaks of
the compulsion of that love that drives Him
onwards to the Cross and says that the Son of Man
must needs suffer, they reply through their
spokesman, "Far be it from Thee, Lord." His
answer is harsh in its kindness: "Get thee behind
Me, Satan." He would have them know without
alternative, that the love that will not suffer is not
worthy of His disciples. Some follow Him for
bread, others because of His mighty deeds of
healing, others of nobler temper because they
hope it will be He who will redeem Israel, and best
of all some follow Him who love greatly like the
Magdalen, because they have sinned and sorrowed
greatly, and have been forgiven. To one and all,
to the bread seekers and to the kingdom seekers
alike, He says, "If any one will come after Me,
let him renounce himself." He will tolerate no
mere insurance of their future. Love of Him
must be uncalculating. "Let him take up his
cross and follow Me"—that is what Infinite
Love demands of mortal love.

This means that a love that will not discipline

itself for service has no place in the plan of Jesus
for the redemption of the world. In His great
intercession He pleads that as for our sakes He
consecrated Himself, so we ourselves also may be
consecrated in truth. He thus teaches us that
we must tread the same pathway of discipline if
we would realise His prayer that we may be one
in Him, that the world may believe that the Father
hath sent Him. Surely, if ever since He lived
among men the world needed the witness of those
who are one in His great purpose of redemption at
the cost of sacrifice, it is in this era of tragedy,
sorrow and disillusionment.

*O Lord Jesus, compelled by the irresistible
power of Thy Love, we ask Thee to accept the Love
which we yield Thee in return. We have nothing
else to give Thee, for all we have is Thine. Even
when our full hearts yield their tribute, we do but
give Thee back Thine own, Thou King of Love.
We cast ourselves before Thy Cross and kiss Thy
pierced Feet, and wash them with our tears, and
yet our love is all unworthy of Thine own. Help
us to prove our love for Thee by loving those whom
Thou hast loved. As Thy Love followed us in our
wrong-doing and again and again raised us when
we fell, so may our love for Thee send us forth
upon the search for every wandering child of Thine.
Inspired by this Love may we rejoice to share Thy
reproach in the world, and by surrender to Thy*

will and by faithful service do what in us lies to
bring all men to the knowledge of Thy Love.
Hear us, our Lord and Master, for Thy name's
sake. Amen.

Our love for Jesus must find expression in our
love for the world. If we in truth love Jesus for
Himself, we shall love all for Jesus. The vision
of the Crucified would be in vain if it did not
inspire us with the purpose of the Cross. "I, if
I be lifted up, will draw all men unto Me"; and
yet to-day the whole flock is scattered abroad.

The last and greatest attempt in history to
unite the nations by force of arms, inspired by
hatred, pride, and self-seeking has left the world
in ruins. If we would "build again Jerusalem"
—the City of God—in all lands, the Law of Love
for all mankind must rule and discipline us. The
heavenly vision which changed the life of Saul of
Tarsus must drive us forth as he was driven forth
to those of whom the Voice said, "Unto whom
now I send thee." That vision in the years to
follow made his rule to be "I buffet my body
and bring it into subjection, lest after having
preached to others, I myself should be a castaway."

The compelling force in the lives of all the
saints has been the vision of the Crucified. The
method of their lives trained them to endure
hardness as good soldiers of Jesus Christ. We
shall find in our study of the record of those who

have pre-eminently become one with our Lord
in His redeeming work that they owe their spiritual
primacy in each age to the strength which has been
the product of discipline, and to the discipline which
has been the fruit of their passionate love of Jesus.

It has become common in these days to dismiss
lightly, almost contemptuously, Archdeacon
Paley's insistence on the evidential value of the
fact that men were willing to endure hardship
and martyrdom as witnesses to the Resurrection.
We may find a stronger argument in the universal
testimony of believers that the power of faith in a
risen Saviour has changed their lives, and in the
existence of the Living Church all through the
centuries. But this must not lead us to overlook
the fact that the Church can only live and exercise
its redeeming mission, if it be animated by the
passion of a consuming love for Jesus, and because
of that love, repeats the renunciation of self which
marked the birth of the Church. The world, after
the great war of the twentieth century, is in as
urgent need of apostles and apostolic methods as
it was after the destruction of Jerusalem in the
first century.

Archimedes declared that with a fulcrum he
could move the world. In these pages it has been
sought to show from the teaching of the Saints,
that they have found in love and self-surrender
such a spiritual fulcrum.

It is important that the lover of Jesus should understand that he is not called upon to be singular in sacrificing many desirable things to attain a greater end. If we consult the kings of the market and ask them how they accumulated millions by the sale of common things, they will answer that, to attain what they regarded as success, they endured hard discipline and

How the Passions Discipline Men

"scorned delights, and lived laborious days."

Possessed by the passion for wealth, they wasted neither time nor money in frivolities. It is no mere accident that the household names attached to common things are names that were once held in high esteem among the Puritans, the Quakers, and the Methodists. It was in homes ruled by the teaching of George Fox, John Wesley, and the great Puritan divines, that the founders of those monopolies learned to sacrifice to the future the pleasures of the moment. The devotion and zeal that made one man a prophet and another an apostle, when diverted into business, made that idol of the nineteenth century—"The Successful Merchant." The children of the Protestants have sacrificed much of the beauty and joy of life to make gigantic fortunes, or like Willian Penn to turn the wilderness and the solitary place into a British colony, or like Livingstone, Speke, and

Grant, to open up the Dark Continent to civilisation. Followers of Jesus Christ have too unhesitatingly and uncritically applauded the sacrifices of merchant princes, explorers and adventurers in the affairs of the world, have made such men peers and well-nigh canonised them.

Jesus, who knew what was in man, attacked the love of money as the first and most evil rival of the love of God; God and Mammon in His teaching were locked in a conflict in which there can be no armistice and no peace until Mammon is overthrown. If He was right, as right He surely was, then there is many a statue in Westminster Abbey and brass tablet in Nonconformist chapels to the memories of those who "by labours more abundant" have made great wealth, which would be more fittingly placed in the Stock Exchange or on the walls of the other markets of that world to which they belong.

Since Jacob underwent those years of discipline and obedience for love of his cousin Rachel, "the maiden passion for a maid" has always in men's history proved its power to subdue the evil and strengthen the good. Those years, followed by the experience of Peniel, changed the Hebrew bargainer who, by trickery and fraud, robbed his brother of his birthright and his uncle of his flocks, into one who "as a prince had power with God and men and prevailed."

It is needless to refer at greater length to the records of what men in all ages have endured for lawful or unlawful love of women:

> "I know
> Of no more subtle master under heaven
> Than is the maiden passion for a maid,
> Not only to keep down the base in man
> But teach high thoughts."

A few minutes' meditation will suffice to bring home to us the moulding influences of passion, and the pains and trials that men will undergo for love of country, love of power, and love of high place among their fellows. The love of country alone had more martyrs for its cause in the Great War than the Christian Church has had in centuries of its history. For love of Fatherland, almost countless thousands have left father, mother, children, and home, and have gladly endured hard training for months and years. They have gone forth to death or victory without a thought of self. The trenches of Flanders, Gallipoli, and Mesopotamia call us with no uncertain note to prove by our lives that our care for the triumph of the Kingdom of God is as real as was theirs for the victory of their country and the right as they saw it.

Blessed Lord, Who has taught us that the children of this world are in their generation wiser than the children of light, shame us by

*the example of their zeal for the things that perish
in the using. Thou, our Master, for Love of us
didst go forth to face the trials and temptations of the
wilderness. So may we be driven by the impulse
of Thy loving spirit to seek joyfully the discipline
of the desert, that we may have courage to bear
the cross of following Thee. May we be as
untiring and unresting in our efforts for the
spread of the Kingdom, as are the money changers
in the pursuit of gain. May our vision of the
Love that led Thee along the hard and stony road
from Nazareth to Calvary compel us to give up
self-indulgence and all desire to win the praise of
men, that we may share Thy purpose of winning
the world from sin. Amen.*

Passionate sympathy with his own people drove
Moses to slay the Egyptian oppressor, and sent
him forth from the pleasures of the King's court
**Example
from the Old
Testament** to the discipline of a shepherd's
life in Midian. In those years of
loneliness his love for the oppressed
was creating by this discipline the man
for whom the common bush should be aflame with
God, and whom the solitude should help to understand the anger of God against the Egyptian
tyrant. The sacrifice of Moses made him the
successful antagonist of the Great King, and the
creator of a nation out of a horde of slaves. But

to learn the true greatness of his mission he had yet to spend long days in fasting and communion with the Infinite, whence he came forth as the law-giver, who should mould a nation's destiny and character.

Moses from Pisgah, and Elijah from Horeb, looked forward to the hope of Israel. Sorrow for the sins of his people, the gross immoralities of the worship of Baal and Astarte, drove Elijah in fasting and prayer to the desert of Horeb. There he was given new courage to face the wrath of the King, and moral strength to destroy the cult of those false gods.

The young Hebrews in captivity refused the rich meats from the table of the great King, and by discipline created a character which gave them courage to say, in as brave words as ever men spoke, "Be it known unto thee, O King . . . Our God is able to deliver us out of the burning fiery furnace, but *if not*, we will not worship thy gods."

In a like spirit and with a like purpose, Daniel thrice opened his windows towards Jerusalem and prayed in defiance of the King's commands. "Losing his life" for love of his God and country, he saved it to become the prophet prince, whose example should be the inspiration of his race in their long years of captivity and exile.

Great as was the zeal of these men and the inspiration that came to them through the trials and labours which they underwent, "God has provided some better thing for us."

The Bridegroom had been taken away, and the children of the Bridechamber fasted as they waited in the upper room for the promised gift of God's Spirit. The Church, which is His Bride, in her hours of greatest faith, waits for His appearing with confidence and hope. But since the cloud received Him out of her sight, how grievously has she been wounded by those who should have loved her best! Torn by the evil passions of those who bear her name, her children filled with hot anger against each other, her heart is racked with sorrow for the woes of those He loves, and with great longing she waits for the Lord. The Son of Man wept over Jerusalem as He foresaw that her enemies would come up against her. We who have not the spiritual insight to foresee as He foresaw, can look back and see in retrospect enough to drive us to weep for the sins and sorrows of men everywhere in the years that are just past.

It was surely no accident that the two great souls whose prayers and fellowship sustained Jesus on the Mountain in the hour of His need, should be the two who, like Him, had each spent forty days in communion with God, as they prepared for their life's work. The consciousness of what He must

The Discipline of Love in Fasting

suffer "of the elders and chief priests and scribes"
had just burst out in His teaching and brought upon
Him the rebukes of those whom He loved, but
who did not yet understand Him.   And from these
men He turned to the hero spirits of the past who
had known in some degree, as He knew it, a passion
for souls which had driven each of them to those
days of fasting and prayer and communion with
God.

Millions cry to us to-day from their sorrow or
their sin, "Who will show us any good?"   We
cannot err as we seek to answer them, if we follow
Moses, Elijah, and Jesus in the method of training
for this task.   The disciples who were not yet
worthy to join in the mysterious fellowship of
the Mount had no answer to give to the man at
the foot of the mountain who cried for help.

Fasting brings us into fellowship with Jesus
in all that He endured in those forty days of preparation in the wilderness; and it also creates in
us a sense of unity with the great saints of all the
ages who have sorrowed with the sorrow of their
Lord, and have passed through the discipline that
sorrow brings, to the victory of faith.   Moses,
Elijah, Jesus teach the same lesson of triumph
through discipline.   Obedience learned through
suffering has been taught all through the centuries
in the Christian Church, by Paul, Francis, Wesley,
and all who have handed on the succession

of the living Church.   Life only comes through sacrifice.

The fasting inspired by love is also the means by which God's children in all ages have subdued and kept in check those passions which, when disciplined and matured, have been transmuted into energy for God's service. We may often see, flowing over some mountain side from the melting glacier above, that liberated mountain torrent which is pouring forth unused its great store of energy. A few years later we come back to that same track, and find that this force has been captured for the service of man. Thus does the love that melts the glaciers in our souls set free those forces of our being that may burst forth in harm and injury, or pass away in mere wasteful tumult, or be disciplined and used for love's purpose in the world. Until the pride of the Pharisee on the road to Damascus had been subdued by the vision of Love Crucified, the stoning of Stephen was the natural expression of that great energy which in later years crossed from continent to continent in its passion to save. The sins of the young Augustine, and the profligacy of Francis of Assisi in his early days, were the wasteful outpourings of forces that in manhood, under the Discipline of Love, did the Master's will.

The disciples went forth from Calvary and

Olivet with a message of gladness in realised hope,
that hurried them across all frontiers, taking no
heed of differences of race and nation, that they
might tell all men of the Love of God.   The
greatness of their mission, as it burst upon them in
the revelation of Pentecost, called them, as it calls
us to-day, to stop at no sacrifice to make known
the unsearchable riches of Christ.

Fasting will be helpful to us as we realise its
sacramental character, and pass through the
material to the spiritual.   It is an outward and
visible expression of sorrow for all the ingratitude
and failure that has marked our service to our
Lord.   There can be no more thought of "merit"
in fasting than there is in the tears of the little
child that has fallen down and cries in its pain.   It
is the demerit—the sin—that drives us to the
expression of our sorrow.   The Bridegroom has
been taken, therefore the Children of the Bridechamber fast.   Our sins have separated us from
God, therefore in penitence and fasting we cry
"Lord, lift Thou up again upon us the light of
Thy countenance."

It is not, therefore, a matter for wonder that the
Church, with an unbroken voice throughout all
the ages, has called her members to the discipline
of self in fasting.   The Forty Days which lead us
in the Church's year through the sorrows of
Calvary to the joys of Easter, have been observed

through all the centuries as days for this spiritual discipline. And those who are the children of the revival of the eighteenth century with all its tendency to react against forms and ceremonies have yet retained in the Methodist service book the beautiful collect for Lent:

O Lord, Who for our sake didst fast forty days and forty nights, give us grace to use such abstinence that, the flesh being subdued to the Spirit, we may ever obey Thy godly motions in righteousness and true holiness. Amen.

When we read the sentence, "And Jesus went up into a mountain to pray," and are told that He remained all night alone in communion with His Father, it is as though the Evangelist opened a window into the soul of Jesus and flashed a light thereon that we might read of the greatness of His Love. He has been wearied on the lowland by His incessant acts of healing the bodies and souls of men. When most conscious that virtue has gone out of Him, that the message full of grace and truth has exhausted the Preacher, that the deeds done in mercy have made His human nature cry out for rest, Love drives Him up into the mountain to pray. Even the Son of God finds a distraction in His mission of mercy that can only be corrected in silence and alone with the Father.

The Discipline of Love in Prayer

We pause in adoring wonder at the Love that thus "emptied itself" for us men and for our salvation. But while we marvel at the greatness of divine compassion and rejoice therein, let us not miss the lesson which these facts should teach to everyone who seeks to follow Him. When we are most wearied by the world, and perplexed by the sorrows we have sought to relieve, then does our love of God and men call us to the solitude—"up into the mountain to pray." We must learn that the moment when earth has drained us of all strength is Heaven's opportunity to help us. Wounded in the house of our friends, exhausted with the cares and trials of the day, tired out by the changing problems of life, we learn to understand the blessed paradox of the call to the weary— "Take my yoke upon you . . . and ye shall find rest unto your souls."

This is the key to the discipline of prayer. The last effort of the soldier who has been fighting all day the battle of the Cross must be to climb up into the secret places of the Most High that he may rest under the shadow of the Almighty. The first act of returning consciousness after the rest of night must be to lift up our eyes to the hills from whence cometh our help. Thus shall the evening and the morning make up the new day of the soul's life.

Prayer is the natural and inevitable expression

of love, but it is not therefore easy; it remains
the supreme discipline of the soul. If we turn
to the greatest cry of penitence which is recorded
in the spiritual annals of our race, the fifty-first
Psalm, we listen to one who agonises in his grief
for his sin, who wrestles with the memory of
temptation yielded to, that he may cast himself
upon that great loving kindness, that he may
rejoice in the multitude of those tender
mercies.

In the seventeenth chapter of St. John, the
Beloved Disciple draws aside the veil, that we
may see and hear how Jesus prayed. There can
be no question, as we hear the voice of Love in that
great prayer, that the final expression of that Love
was found naturally and inevitably in the Cross.
That is what prayer meant to Jesus, and if we
would train ourselves to be fellow workers with
Him we must learn to pray as He prayed.

Our fathers had power with God and man and
prevailed because of that constant wrestling in
prayer, which is the soul's highest discipline. We
cannot follow the great saints as they followed
Christ, unless love drives us, compels us, forces us
to the wrestling ground of intercessory prayer.

There is a temptation to become selfish and self-
centred even in our prayers to God. The corruption of the best thing is the worst. The prayer of
the Pharisee is the abyss of selfishness. The

intercessory prayer of Jesus is history's highest note of self-sacrifice.

Our knowledge of the Love of God to us calls us to pray for ourselves that we may be worthy of His Love. Our love for Jesus as it unites us to Him and makes His prayers one with ours, will lead us to intercessory prayer for all men. The prayer in which we draw nearest to our Lord is the one in which even our own soul's needs are least remembered; when we are filled with the desire that the Will of God may be done, and the Kingdom of God may be established in the hearts of all men. In this common prayer, our petitions are united with His, and with those of the saints in all ages, who have toiled and struggled for the victory of the good and true. Thus prayer rises from its worst possibilities of a mere individual desire to propitiate an angry deity, and becomes a part of that mingled praise and intercession which rises from the Holy Church throughout all the world, and from the Church Triumphant in the presence of the Redeemer.

O Saviour of the World, Who didst prepare Thyself for Thine agony and bloody sweat, Thy Cross and Passion, by communion with the Father, help us each to take up our own Cross and follow Thee. When we are weary with the cares and anxieties of life, do Thou so quicken us with the sense of Thy presence that we may

*find rest in Thee. In silence, and alone with
Thee, let us hear Thy voice telling us of our high
calling, and making plain to us how we may
obey Thy call. In penitence and love may we
rejoice in the greatness of Thy forgiveness and go
forth from Thy secret place with faith and strength
renewed to do Thy will in all things. As Thou
dost help our weakness in this our prayer, so help
us day by day to live as we pray, for Thy Name's
sake. Amen.*

Of all the names that have been given to the
Feast of Love, the Blessed Eucharist is in many
ways the most expressive. The Greek
word "Giving of Thanks" most surely
The Disci- expresses the attitude of all who are
pline of privileged to receive from their Lord
Love in the Broken Body and the Shed Blood
the Holy by which they have been bought. It
Communion
may therefore seem that this is not the place of
discipline. It is in the words of my old Professor,
Dr. Findlay, "the Trysting Place of the Lover and
the Beloved." But love calls for sacrifice, and
"here we offer and present ourselves, our souls and
bodies, to be a reasonable, holy, and living sacrifice." If we not only commemorate the sacrifice
of Calvary, but also thus offer ourselves, then
indeed this union with our Lord in sacrificial
purpose needs the highest effort of the Christian

life, and herein we shall find the discipline for further service.

If this be true, as so many thousands of our fellow Christians are finding it to be true to-day, let us for our soul's need respond to John Wesley's appeal for "constant communion." In the closing years of his great evangelical mission, he urges his followers not to be content merely with "frequent communion," but "constantly" to use this supreme means of grace.

Life gives few occasions of respite from its storm and stress. But here before the Mercy Seat we may bow in silent adoration. In the hard pressure of life it is so difficult to find a real spiritual breathing place. Here in the solemn stillness of the early morning, whilst yet the dew makes all things fresh and our energies are still unwearied by the cares of life, it is possible to pray as at no other hour of the day. Here we have power, or it is given to us, to discipline the wandering thought, and to concentrate all our desires on our union with the Crucified, "that we may know Him and the fellowship of His sufferings." In those sacred moments grace is given us to say from our hearts:

> Soul of Christ, sanctify me,
> Body of Christ, save me;
> Blood of Christ, inebriate me,
> Passion of Christ, strengthen me.

We return from the Mount to the plains with this blessed message—"He that eateth My Flesh and drinketh My Blood dwelleth in Me and I in Him." The mere act of giving to our Lord and to the contemplation of His dying love the best hour of the day, has brought its own response in the effective discipline of unruly thoughts and desires.

God has given to each of us a great gift in the imagination. Thereby the lover in exile comforts himself when separated from his **The Disci-** beloved. The great saints in all ages **pline of** to whom God has given the power of **Love in** expression by pen or brush have left **Meditation** us the legacy of the vision of God in Christ which has been granted to them. But when the Reformation separated the Reformers from the corruptions which had grown up in the Church, they forgot the parable of the tares and the wheat. The zeal of Luther and Calvin, Knox and the Puritans, uprooted many evils, but lost in so doing much of great value. For centuries their children have been deprived of great gifts of genius by which saints, whether artist, poet, or writer in prose, had enriched the world. The corruption of monasteries and convents had been condemned by many a reformer within the Church before Luther was born. But the pity of it was that in the zeal for purity which the men of the

sixteenth century shared with many saints inside
and heretics outside, during the whole history of
the Church, great fruits of meditation were lost to
the children of the Reformers. The habit of
meditation itself, because it has been practised
by hermits and monastic communities largely
passed out of the experience of Northern Europe,
to the great loss of the nations. Yet nowhere does
the discipline of love find greater opportunity
for the culture of the soul than in that concentra-
tion of thought upon our Lord's gift of Himself
which finds its expression alike in the paintings of
a Fra Angelico and the poetry of the two Bernards
of Cluny and Clairvaux, or in these later days, of
Charles Wesley and F. W. Faber. These men, and
all in every age whose thought has enriched the
Church with some new presentation of the Love of
the Redeemer, meditated long and earnestly, and
in this matter, as in many others, we have entered
into their labours. Whatever the defects in the
teaching of George Fox, the early Quakers did
something to recall us to the Catholic practice of
meditation for the disciplining of the soul.

Our experience in the Holy Communion teaches
us that what is best in a meeting of the Society of
Friends is found when we kneel in adoration of the
Love we celebrate in the still hours of the morning.
It is in silence that we hear the voice of the
Eternal. Moses alone on Sinai learns of the

righteousness which exalts a nation. When Elijah obeys the command, "Go forth and stand upon the mount before the Lord," then the still small voice gives him new courage for his conflict with Baal. It is our duty to get alone with God, if in this crowded age we would save our souls. The Psalmist lived and wrote in a land that was not cursed with six newspaper editions in a day. Even he in his desire that his "eyes might be opened that he might behold wondrous things out of God's law," says, "At midnight I will rise to give thanks to Thee"; "I prevented the dawning of the morning that I might meditate on Thy word." The Love of God impels him to find in the solitude of the night the hour for the teaching of the soul. We must find the wilderness somewhere in our lives if we would have strength to conquer the world and to give God's message.

There is nothing that is wrong in essence in the evening newspapers, the converse of the crowd, the cinematographic movement of to-day. It is the pace, the rush, the crowding, the noise of the century that gives no chance for our soul's culture unless we compel it. Love shuns the multitude. Love asks to be alone with us. "Could ye not watch with Me one hour?" was said not merely once, long, long ago, in a garden of olives, but is the cry of the Lord of love in our hearts to-day. Jesus and the great saints have left the record of their "colloquies"—He with His Father, and they with Him. In the fourth book of the Imitation is that great colloquy between the Beloved and the Disciple which John Wesley printed for his people in their "Guide to the Altar." Let us get away from the ceaseless chatter of the crowd, that we may talk with God for the strengthening of our souls. This is no mere mediæval "tradition of men." It is the common privilege of all who love our Lord.

> "Talk with us, Lord, Thyself reveal
> Whilst here o'er earth we rove,
> Speak to our hearts and let us feel
> The kindling of Thy love."

It was in that fashion that the saints of other days learned "the mind that is in Christ." It was no mere ascetic punishment of self that drove men into the solitude to be alone with God. Jesus went to the mountain alone, because the Father "loved Him before the foundation of the world." The souls who have quickened the life of the Church in all ages have disciplined themselves in the great silence, and have spoken with their Lord because He also loved them before time began.

The object of language is to convey thought. **The Athletes of the Faith** A conventional heading for this section would have been "Christian Ascetics," but like many conventions it would have hidden the truth. When St. Paul used

the verb ἀσκῶ (Acts xxiv. 16), from which
is derived the word ἀσκητής he had a very
definite picture in his mind's eye of the trained
athlete and the training he underwent in order
to fight in the games, or to run in the races
of the world of his day. The man who stands
ready to fight, to wrestle, to run, with every
muscle hardened, with every nerve alert, the master
of himself, is his ideal for all who would follow
Jesus. The word *athlete* is simply the Greek word
ἀσκητής rightly translated. The ἀσκητής is the
trained athlete who "fought with beasts at
Ephesus," or "ran the race set before him" in
the stadium at Olympia. He was as far removed
from the Hindu dervish or fakir as man could be.
He knew the joy of life, as his red blood coursed
rapidly through every artery, when he faced his
foe or ran his race. There was no crippling of
self as in the case of the Hindu dervish, but the
fullest possible development of his power. His
self-denial was akin to that of the member of the
'Varsity Eight who understands so well the meaning of the words, "Rejoice, O young man, in thy
youth, and let thine heart cheer thee in the days
of thy youth." To the athlete, the victory is
worth all the discipline, all the training, all
the self-denial. A member of the "Eight," or
any Oxford or Cambridge "blue," or an Olympic
wrestler who shrank from rigidly obeying his

trainer's instructions, would be despised by all his fellows. "They do it to obtain a corruptible crown."

The Church of the twentieth century dreads the discipline of the athlete of the first century, the confessor, the martyr, and the saint. The world turns away from the teaching of these upon whom their faith makes such slight demands, and passes the Church of the spiritual unrealities to go to the cinema with its pictures of real battlefields. There was colour and life in the arena and on the stadium. St. Paul found the same elements in the battle of the faith. To him this meant, not sadness, but joy. "Rejoice evermore" is his motto like the *gaudeamus* of the Etonians on their festival day.

The Church of this century is in the main grey, dull, and without appeal to a generation that has faced living realities as scarce any other generation in the world's history has done. A cold, colourless, ethereal Christianity will never call men to high adventure. Let us at least ask of ourselves and others the moral passion and earnestness, and consequent self-denial, of the ancient gladiators and the modern athlete.

Pride is the darling sin of many excellent patriots. On August 4, 1914, not one in a thousand of the followers of Thomas Cranmer and Martin Luther would have hesitated to confess his pride. Most of them would have avowed it.

Pride and Vanity

And yet pride is indeed one of the deadly sins. From Lucifer to Nebuchadnezzar the Hebrew Scriptures are full of the ruin wrought by pride. The personal, social, and national pride of the Pharisees brought Jesus and John the Baptist at once into collision with them and their teaching. "God is able even of these stones to raise up children unto Abraham," was a bitter blow to their pride of race. "Ye compass sea and land to make one proselyte, and when he is made, ye make him threefold more the child of hell than yourselves," is the stern rebuke for all time against sectarian pride and bigotry. "Lowliness of mind" (ταπεινοφροσύνη) is a word rarely found outside the New Testament. If and when men truly believe that the Son of God emptied Himself of the Divine glory, then only is it possible by the standard of the Cross, rightly to judge the prizes and honours of this life. So also is it true that the divisions of Christendom which curse the world to-day are condemned as we look upon the Crucified.

He has prayed that "all may be one," but the pride of His followers has defeated the prayer. For centuries it has seemed true that:

> "West is West and East is East,
> And never the twain shall meet."

The Greek Orthodox defeats love's purpose in

his pride by his scorn for the first heretic—the Pope, and all his followers. The Latins reply by leaving the city of Constantine and the cathedral of Justinian to be captured and held by the Turk, whilst Western Christendom looks idly on.

The divisions of Christendom have gravely affected the Peace of Versailles at several points. The rivalries of sects interfere with love's purpose in the redemption of the world, and these things spring from pride.

I am writing these lines in Switzerland at the open window, five thousand feet above the sea. The sun is shining brightly on a billowy sea of cloud one thousand feet below. Beyond this cloud-sea stretches the whole range of the Pennine Alps from Mont Blanc to the Matterhorn; the mountain peaks stand out in all their grandeur and beauty on such a cloudless day as this.

Three days since I was on the lower level travelling under the canopy of mist. No vision of glory greeted my eyes, but all was dull and dark and damp. It is no merit of the traveller that he is in the sunshine to-day when yesterday he was in the mist. So in the spiritual world, it is not right and fitting that those who have had glimpses of the glory of their Lord, who have heard the Heavenly chorus—"Lift up your heads, O ye gates, and be ye lifted up ye everlasting doors, and let the King of Glory come in"—should find

cause for pride in their privileges, or scorn those
who have never shared them.

St. Paul, to whom had come a great revelation
which no words could express, tells us that the
Lord whom he loved so greatly sent a messenger
of Satan to buffet him lest he should be exalted
above measure. He gives us the warning, "Mind
not high things." Let not the mystic to whom is
given some hidden secret of the Love of his Lord
scorn those who have not shared his privilege. Let
not the one who finds in the outward forms of the
Church a means of revealing to him spiritual
truths condemn those to whom these forms have
no such meaning. Let not him, to whom the
gift of a great intellect has made many things plain
which are obscure to those who are not thus gifted,
fail to remember the great truth that Jesus taught,
"Thou hast hidden these things from the wise
and prudent, and hast revealed them unto babes.
Even so, Father, for so it seemed good in Thy sight."

The Master uses temptations to humble us,

The Disci-
pline of
Love in
Temptation

not because He desires to see us in
the dust, but that He may exalt us
again in due season. "Satan hath
desired to have you that he may sift
you as wheat, but I have prayed for thee that
thy faith fail not," is the message that we recall
sometimes when we have been over-burdened by
the things of time and sense, the temptations of

the world in which we live, and have yielded
to temptation, and had to go back in lowly
penitence to seek forgiveness. Shall we sin
that grace may abound? God forbid, but as
we are humbled by our failures, and our own
forgetfulness of the source from whence all strength
must come, we must recognise that it is love that
teaches us through the discipline of failure our
own weakness, and our own dependence upon the
strength which He alone can impart.

It is needful that we should warn ourselves of
a great danger to the spiritual life. Let us
remember that those who were most
The Disci- religious in the time of our Lord's
pline of ministry, who prayed and fasted to
Love and the knowledge of all men, were those
the Danger
of Hypocrisy whose lives He condemned most un-
sparingly.

For every form of religion the danger of hypocrisy exists. We are always threatened with the
possibility that our religious observances and even
the memory of our deepest spiritual experiences
will, if our communion with Christ be broken,
become a mere skeleton of a dead past, which we
shall instinctively hide from ourselves and our
fellows. This is a danger in all phases of the
religious life. In a religion which is institutional,
forms and ceremonies may exist without any
spiritual reality behind them; but the danger

is equally great in a religious life which is
experimental, mystical, and emotional. We
talk or write of the experience of yesterday
in the hope that it will return to-morrow. Then
at once we create a mask behind which we hide
a separation from Christ, which is the more real
and fatal because it is hidden. Emotions which
have stirred us deeply may be recalled to memory
with fatal ease, without any of the power to lead
us to discipline and fellowship with our Lord
which they once possessed. The great mystical
experience of St. Paul, the unspeakable revelations
which he received, did not prevent him from declaring his need of constant discipline lest he should
become a castaway.

These lessons are impressed upon us as we read
the lives of the three sons of Catherine de' Medici
who became Kings of France. The complete
divorce in them of the devotional and the ethical
is typical of what may happen to all Christians
who cease for one moment the endeavour to live
as they pray.

That great philanthropist, St. Vincent de Paul,
has put this warning in words that apply to such
devotees as Anne of Austria, the mother of Louis
XIV, and equally to Christians of all ranks.

"If you are seeking fine ideas in your prayer
and amusing yourself with complicated thoughts
—particularly when you do this with the intention

of advertising yourself when you are giving an account of your prayer—you are guilty of a sort of blasphemy. In fact, you are making an idol of yourself, for in your intercourse with God your object is to foster self-complacency; you are using time that should be sacred for your own satisfaction. In flattering yourself that you have beautiful sentiments, you are offering a sacrifice to the idol of your own vanity. In prayer let self become nothing, and when we speak of our prayer, let us relate our thoughts humbly; and if there are any that seem to us fine, let us be distrustful of them and afraid, lest they were suggested by vainglory or the devil himself. And because there is always this possibility, directly we think we have a fine inspiration we must humble ourselves utterly, whether it comes to us in prayer or when we are preaching or when we are talking to others."

On another occasion he observed that it was better to be incapable of anything but the simplest form of prayer, and to be diligent in the correction of one's faults, than to go into spiritual ecstasies and to speak evil of one's neighbour.

And yet again, in his advice to his mission priests, he writes, "How may we hope to do our work? How can we lead souls to God? How can we stem the tide of wickedness among the people? How can we instil the idea of virtue and discipline

in those who are entrusted to our care? The
most important point of all is that we should
have real touch with our Lord in prayer. When
we are in any doubt turn instantly to God and say,
'Lord, Who art the source of knowledge, teach
me what I ought to do in this matter.' And
further we must turn to God in prayer to preserve
in our own souls the love and the fear of Him, for
alas! it is necessary that we should know that
many who intend to bring others to salvation come
to destruction themselves. To avoid this we must
be so closely united to our Lord that we cannot
lose Him, lifting up heart and soul towards Him
constantly, and saying, 'Lord, do not suffer that
I myself should fall in trying to save others. Lead
me Thyself, and do not withhold from me the grace,
that by means of me, Thou hast given to others.'"

I have quoted at such length from his words,
because the need of France after the Fronde
rebellion in the regency of Anne of Austria, with
that tortuous Italian, Mazarin, as her counsellor,
was not greater than the need of the world to-day,
with its social unrest, its dangers from a violently
atheistic Socialist republic in the East, and from
a materialistic plutocracy in the West. In
such a city as Paris was in the middle of the
seventeenth century, Vincent de Paul was hailed as
"Father of his country," and even in the Paris
of to-day his statue at the corners of the streets

tells the poor where they may find that their needs
are met. At the end of a career of unbroken
service to his nation, his life-long endeavour is
thus summed up, *"Ruinez en moi, Seigneur, tout
ce qui vous y déplaît."* From the words of this
practical mystic comes the warning that there is
a real danger of a divorce between the ethical and
the religious. "Be ye therefore perfect, even as
your Father which is in Heaven is perfect." St.
Luke expresses it, "Be ye therefore merciful."
"I and My Father are one." "Perfect in love" is
the standard He sets before us. This is the mark
to which St. Paul "presses forward" with that
persistent discipline of self, that consuming energy,
of the explorer of the unknown depths of perfect
love. The Beloved Disciple in his letters of love
to the Church is the sacred writer who most
realises that the lust of the flesh, the lust of the eye,
and the pride of life must be entirely subdued if the
reign of Jesus is to be fully established in our hearts.

We must "declare the whole counsel of God,"
as we call men to obey the Gospel rule and
discipline themselves until sin is conquered. The
thought that this is our message, that there is no
escape from it, is a burden that can only be borne, if
in silent communion with the Lord whom we love we
wait for Him to say, "My grace is sufficient for thee."

*O Lord Jesus, we praise Thee not only that Thou
hast redeemed us from our sins by Thine own most*

precious blood, but also that in Thy life, full of
grace and truth, Thou has left us an example that
we should follow in Thy footsteps. Help us by
the constant inspiration of Thy Holy Spirit to
conquer all that is sinful in our lives, and as we
love Thee, to love what Thou dost desire, and
hate the things that Thou dost hate. May every
chain that binds us to this world be broken by
Thy Love, and· thus make us worthy when these
days of trial are ended, to enter into the full joy
of Thy presence, our Lord and our Redeemer.

These are the lessons learned in seven decades of
a crowded life. None can escape from the need
of discipline. All depends for our-
Conclusion selves, and something for the world,
upon how we accept the teaching of the years as
they pass. "The tale that is told" will soon be
completed for the youngest as well as the oldest.
Penitence and sorrow for failures must find a
place in the retrospect of every honest judge of his
own life. If we are led thereby to strenuous
endeavour, to master ourselves and bring our best
to Him Who has loved us with so great a Love,
there is still time and opportunity to share in our
Lord's redemptive work. Men may pass heedlessly
by the Cross, but its message was never more needed.
There is a great darkness over all lands, but out
of the Three Hours' darkness came the cry of the

Redeemer—"It is finished." The wounds of the great conflict are many and grievous. Lives have been cut short which might have quickened mankind by their devotion and zeal. To us who remain the task is the greater because they have been taken away, and we are the weaker through all the strain of these terrible years. Looking to ourselves we are driven to cry out, "Who is sufficient for these things?" But if we forget ourselves in the greatness of the work, "our sufficiency is of God," and we are able to go forward with courage. Again and again, men whom He has called to deliver a great message have said, "I am a man of unclean lips." But the live coal from off the altar of consecration has touched their lips, and enabled them to speak with "fire of love." The world is waiting for a message, and if we are given boldness "to declare the whole counsel of God," men will heed our words and turn to do the will of our Father. Amid all the bitterness of the counsels of men, the gracious message of Calvary remains unchanged. Despite the wreck of a world in ruins, let us go forward in faith, hope, and love knowing that we "seek a city which hath foundations whose builder and maker is God." United in the bond of faith, in the confidence of hope, in the assurance of love, let us rejoice that he who fights with Omnipotence on his side must gain the final victory.

Chapter VI

THE VISION OF GOD

It is in harmony with the facts of the Christian life that we should pass directly from thoughts on the Discipline of Love to consider what the ages teach us about the Vision of God. In his notable Bampton lectures on *The Vision of God*, a mine from which I have quarried many thoughts, Dr. Kirk quotes what Socrates then said as illustrating the Pagan anticipations that prepared mankind for the message for which the whole world, Jewish and Greek alike, was waiting. The double purpose for which the Church was to be called into being by our Lord was to offer men the vision of God and to bid them pursue that vision. It is an anticipation of that message that Socrates, describing his unforgettable experiences as an initiate into the mysteries of Eleusis, says: "We beheld the beatific vision, and were initiated into a mystery which may be truly called blessed." He goes on to speak of those who with himself each "according to the

measure of his abilities is always clinging to the
recollection of those things in which God abides,
and in beholding which He is what He is. And he
who employs aright those memories is ever being
initiated into perfect mysteries and alone becomes
truly perfect. . . ." "He forgets earthly interests
and is rapt in the divine . . . and when he sees
the beauty of earth, is transported with the
recollection of true beauty." In striking passages
Socrates links together the vision of God, the
word of God, the imitation of God and the
spiritual well-being of our fellow men. "They
seek a love who is to be made like Him whom
they serve, and when they have found Him,
they themselves imitate their God, and per-
suade their love to do the same."

As we read these words and remember how
much that Plato records as sayings of Socrates is

**Plato and
S. Paul**
Plato's own thought and teaching, we
realise the truth of what Dean Inge
said in a recent lecture: "Plato lighted
a candle which has never been put out, and he
lighted it in Athens." To Plato, as Dr. Inge
expressed it, "the soul is a *lover*. Heavenly love,
taking more and more the place of earthly passion,
lifts up the soul to the realm of eternal values,
Goodness, Truth and Beauty." He insists in that
lecture that Plato's thought influenced the mind of
the Apostle of the Gentiles when he wrote to the

Hellenistic Jews at Corinth and Colossae, saying:
"The things that are seen are temporal, but the
things which are not seen are eternal." "Here we
see through a glass darkly, but then face to face,"
"We then, beholding as in a glass the glory of the
Lord, are changed into the same image from glory
unto glory," and, finally, "If ye then are risen with
Christ seek those things which are above, where
Christ sitteth at the right hand of God."

The same Vision has inspired the letters of
the Beloved Disciple, who in his exile wrote:
"I, John, saw the holy city, new
S. John Jerusalem, coming down from God
out of Heaven . . . and the city
hath no need of sun . . . for the glory of God did
lighten it, and the Lamb is the light thereof." In
the inspiration of the vision, when his exile ended,
he continued his work in Ephesus and Asia Minor
until nearly the end of the first century of the
Christian Era, when, too weak to preach at
length, he was carried to the place of meeting, and
his whole sermon consisted of those simple but
great words, "Little children, love one another."
The triumphant optimism of his message that the
"leaves of the tree of life" shall be "for the healing
of nations" is bound up with the promise that the
servants of the Lamb "*shall see His face*, and His
name shall be in their foreheads."

Irenaeus, in the second century, summarises

Christian teaching on this subject in one striking

**Irenaeus and
Augustine**

epigram: "The glory of God is the living man, and the life of man is the Vision of God." Two centuries later, Augustine, the greatest of the Church's teachers after St. Paul, took for the motto of his life: "It is good for me to cleave to God." Of him Heiler—now a Lutheran professor at Marburg—has said: "He combines in one person Jeremiah and Plato, Paul and Plotinus, John and Origen, Cyprian and Athanasius." The greatness of St. Augustine is manifested in his attempt to solve the paradox of the irresistibility of the Grace of God, confronted with the free-will of man. He finds his solution in teaching that the essence of grace is *love*, and the essence of man's salvation that he should become *loving*. In love and in love alone can man exercise the freedom which God has given him. "Love enfranchises. Passion enslaves." Augustine never wearies of declaring that God's grace—God's love—has an irresistible power to summon forth this love to God which will make man free in the truest and most actual sense of the word. "Love is the power that moves me whithersoever I go." This vivid sense of the compelling love of God leads him onward to his ideal: "The Vision of God in the city of God"— "That most glorious society and celestial city of God's faithful," as he expresses it in the opening words of *de Civitate*. As he contrasts the divine commonwealth with the commonwealth of man he writes: "Two loves, therefore, have given originality to these two cities—self-love in contempt of God with the earthly; love of God in contempt of self with the heavenly. The first seeketh the glory of men and the latter desires God only." The Psalmist expresses this desire when he says: "I shall be satisfied when I awake with Thy likeness."

After all that has been said, it is somewhat startling to be reminded by Dr. Kirk that **S. Bernard and S. Francis** Augustine's description of the vision of God, and all that it implies, contains little that is distinctive of Christianity, and that, "beautiful and exalted as they are," his pages "are all but wholly Platonic." Herein Bernard "shows himself the more truly Christian of the two; the Abbot of Clairvaux completes and transcends the work of the Bishop of Hippo." As has already been emphasised in an earlier chapter, the mission of Saint Bernard was to glorify Jesus in the humanity in which He walked the earth, and to reveal God in the face of Jesus Christ. Eighty years ago, when the ashes of St. Bernard were disinterred, an amulet was found bearing the words: "My beloved is a bundle of myrrh," and that bundle of myrrh is the sum total of the labours and sufferings of Jesus.

"To meditate on these things," says Bernard, "I have called wisdom; in them I find the perfection of righteousness, the fulness of knowledge, the riches of salvation, the abundance of merit. Let Jesus be ever borne, not upon your shoulders as a burden, but before your eyes . . . so shall you easily and readily bear your burdens through His help, Who is the Bridegroom of the Church, above all, God blessed for ever." Dr. Kirk regards Bernard "as no theologian; but of one thing he is certain—moral advance is impossible without the vision of God in Christ. . . . The whole of His teaching is a call for *self*-discipline on the part of his hearers—the self-discipline whose purpose is to see God, and to serve Him."

Nevertheless, we are conscious of a great paradox in the teaching of some of the greatest Christian ascetics. Bernard left Cluny for Clairvaux because the discipline of the older monastery was not sufficiently austere, and yet he warns his monks to beware of "pride in a cassock" and to remember that "spiritual activity is better than bodily mortification." Francis of Assisi, with all his complete renunciation of material wealth, is a true follower of Jesus, in the "sweetness and light" as Matthew Arnold would call it, with which he finds joy in nature, revels in the light of the sun, the song of the birds, and the beauty of fishes. This is, indeed, the supreme paradox of the teaching of

Jesus, that whilst He calls His disciples to follow Him as crossbearers, He yet unfolds to them in His parables a rich panorama of the beauty of His world. A peace which seems to contradict the Cross, steals over the soul, as through the eyes of Jesus we look upon the beauty of lilies, the pearl of great price, the sower scattering the seed, the feast for the returning prodigal, the wine in abundance for the wedding, and, above all, the offer of rest and peace to the weary and heavy laden.

Nevertheless, as Stanley Jones points out in his helpful study of *The Christ of the Mount*, the Beatitudes call for complete renunciation as the necessary precedent to the vision of God, although in the end of the list "leaping for joy we lose ourselves and find our Lord."

To the question, What is the vision of God which Christ promised, in this world in its measure, in the next in its fulness, to the pure in heart? Dr. Kirk replies as follows: "It is confined within no narrow limits; wherever a man's mind has been uplifted, his temptations thwarted, his sorrows comforted, his resolutions strengthened, his aberrations controlled, by the sight of purity, innocence, love, or beauty, such a man has in part the mystical experience. Dim though his mirror may have been, he has yet seen God. . . . So far then from

What is the vision of God?

being rare, the mystical experience is at once the commonest and the greatest of human accidents. . . . What Christianity offers, with its fellowship and its sacraments, its life of prayer and service, its preaching of the Incarnate Son of God, is the same vision in ever increasing plenitude; vouchsafed in such measure as will avail against the worst temptations, the deepest sorrow, the most ingrained self-seeking, and will give constant and daily increase of strength, encouragement and illumination. There is, therefore, no need for us to ask whether we are psychologically capable of seeing God; we have already seen Him."

The Vision of God is set before the Christian as his goal. Our Lord holds it out as the highest blessing offered to the pure in heart, and all teachers of the devout life make purgation the first step to that illumination that floods the soul in the experience of "seeing God." The vision is granted "not of him that willeth, nor of him that runneth, but of God that showeth mercy." So much emphasis has been laid in these pages on the high place of prayer and meditation and discipline in the whole of the life of the soul, that it is essential to insist that, in Augustine's words, though we may "cleanse" the soul by all the actions of a virtuous life, we still depend upon God's goodwill and free beneficence that He may present Himself to our cleared vision, and Himself supply the light

wherein He may be seen. At the same time we
must continually remind ourselves that it is only
in the face of Jesus Christ that we can see God.
It is only by studying the nature of God as revealed
in Jesus Christ that we can prepare ourselves for
the glory of the full vision of God.

This principle of the life of the soul gives the true
emphasis to the importance of systematic meditation on the earthly life, person,
Renunciation and character of our Lord Jesus
leads to the Vision Christ. "That we may know
Him," to use St. Paul's words, "for whom I have
suffered the loss of all things." These are words
from a Pauline meditation on union with Christ.
This is the pathway trodden by all the great saints,
but it is one along which the simplest Christian
can go, that of loving Jesus with the all-compelling
love of St. John, and of Bernard, and of the Curé
d'Ars, and of the brothers Wesley, and of John
Keble, and of all the earnest souls whom we have
known and loved, and who now behold the King
in His glory. As we meditate upon the sufferings
and sacrifice of our Lord, we shall see our own
trials in their true light, not merely as facts to be
borne with resignation, but as the golden opportunities for the exercise of the spirit of renunciation
of which Jesus thought when He said: "If any
man will come after Me, let him deny himself daily
and follow Me." Christ will "work together"

with the soul that thus follows Him in that fellowship of His sufferings and conformity to His death,
which is the only pathway to the renunciation
which He demands in order that through the death
of self we may come with all saints to the enjoyment of that "abundant life," the gift of which to
men was the supreme purpose of the Incarnation.
Thus shall we behold the King in His glory, and at
last enter into the deepest meaning of St. Paul's
great words and know what it is "to be filled with
all the fulness of God."

CHAPTER VII

𝕸𝖊𝖉𝖎𝖙𝖆𝖙𝖎𝖔𝖓𝖘

---

*These outlines will be useful in so far as
they are merely regarded as skeletons and
suggestions for expansion. Each meditation
may occupy any time from five minutes to an
hour, and will, it is hoped, be helpful alike
in private prayer, groups, guilds and classes.
After each sentence there should be a definite
pause.*

A Meditation in Time of Trouble

1. Have mercy upon me, O God, for my soul trusteth in Thee, and in the shadow of Thy wings I will make my refuge until these calamities be overpast.

2. Thou knowest, O Lord, my foolishness, and my sins are not hidden from Thee.

3. O my God, hear me, for Thy waves and Thy billows are gone over me. Save me, O God, for the waters are come in unto my soul. Let not those that wait on Thee be ashamed for my sake, O Lord of Hosts. Let not those that seek Thee lose their way because of me.

4. O hide not Thy face from me for I am in sore trouble. Take me out of the mire that I sink not. Deliver me from the deep waters, and let not the flood drown me. Let not the pit shut her mouth upon me.

5. Answer me, O Lord, for Thy loving kindness is good. Turn Thou unto me according to the multitude of Thy tender mercies. Hide not Thy face from Thy servant, but haste Thee to answer me, and deliver my soul.

6. O God of my salvation, Thou hast been my help. Leave me not, neither forsake me, lest those who love Thee not should say, "There is none to deliver him. God has forsaken him."

7. O my God, be not far from me, but hasten to my help, that I may show Thy strength to this generation and Thy power to everyone that is to come.

8. Thou wilt bring me out of this great trouble. Thou wilt quicken me again, and lead me forth from the depths of the earth. Thou wilt comfort me on every side.

9. Now also when I am old and grey headed, O God forsake me not, until I have showed Thy strength unto this generation, and Thy power to every one that is to come.

10. From the end of the earth will I cry unto Thee, when my heart is overwhelmed. Then Thou wilt lead me to the Rock that is higher than I. Then will I trust myself in the shadow of Thy wings.

11. O my soul, wait thou only upon God. He alone is my hope of salvation, the rock of my strength and my refuge; therefore, in Him will I trust at all times.

12. O my Lord, my trust has been in Thee from my youth. Thy loving kindness has ever surrounded me. Thou hast beset me behind and before with

Thy love, and now in the hour of trial I will praise Thee as I remember all that Thou hast done for me.

13.   How excellent is Thy mercy O God.   It endureth for ever, and Thou wilt not forsake the work of Thine own hand.   My trust is therein for evermore.   Thy mercy is my only hope.   Thou will not disappoint me, O Thou Holy One of Israel. Therefore I will rejoice in Thee at all times, and Thy praise shall continually be in my mouth.

Meditations on the Vision of God in the Face of Jesus Christ

"For God who commanded the light to shine out
of darkness hath shined in our hearts to give
the light of the knowledge of the glory of God
in the face of Jesus Christ."—2 Cor. iv. 6.

(i) By THE MYSTERY OF THY HOLY INCARNATION,
GOOD LORD, DELIVER US.

1. Eternal Word, reveal to us, we beseech
Thee, something of the glory which Thou hadst
with the Father before the world was.

2. Prince of the Kings of the Earth, we rejoice
that of Thine own will Thou didst leave all this
glory and humble Thyself, Thou Lord of all, to
serve those whom Thine Almighty word had called
into being.

3. Blessed and only Potentate, King of Kings,
and Lord of Lords, we marvel at the grace that
laid aside Thine omnipotence to take upon Thee
the weakness of our humanity that Thou mightest
become one with us.

4. Almighty God, Who commandedst the light to shine out of darkness, shine in our hearts to give the light of the knowledge of the glory of God in the face of Thine Incarnate Son.

(ii) By Thy Holy Nativity and Circumcision, Good Lord, deliver us.

1. O Lord, Son of the Highest, we praise Thee because Thou didst humble Thyself to become the son of a Virgin and to be made man for us.

2. O Thou, who art the Heir of all things, and yet didst surrender all for the bareness of the stable and the poverty of the manger, give us the spirit which renounces the gifts of time for the prizes of eternity.

3. Holy Babe of Bethlehem, to Whom the Wise Men brought their offerings of gold and frankincense and myrrh, help us to offer Thee without reserve ourselves, our souls and bodies, to be a reasonable, holy and living sacrifice.

4. Prince of Peace, heralded by the angels, give us grace to lay aside all hatred and prejudice, and whatsoever else doth hinder us from godly union and concord, that we may be united in one holy bond, of truth and peace, of faith and charity, and may with one mind and one mouth glorify Thee.

5. Head of the Church, Who, by Thy Circumcision, didst fulfil the whole law, give us that true circumcision of the spirit which shall enable us to bring all earthly passions into subjection to Thy will.

6. Almighty God, Who commandedst the light to shine out of darkness, shine in our hearts to give the light of the knowledge of the glory of God in the face of Thy Son Who was born in Bethlehem.

(iii) BY THY BAPTISM, FASTING AND TEMPTATION, GOOD LORD, DELIVER US.

1. Lord Jesus Christ, upon Whom the Holy Spirit descended in the waters of Jordan, and Whom the Father claimed as His Beloved Son, help us to hear and heed Thy message as His Ambassador to a world in rebellion against Him.

2. Blessed Lord, as it became Thee, in the baptism of John, to fulfil all righteousness, grant us, who have been baptised into Thy name, to be buried with Thee by baptism into death that henceforth we also may walk in newness of life.

3. O Lord, who for our sakes didst fast forty days and forty nights, give us grace to use such abstinence as shall enable us to subdue the flesh to the spirit, and shall strengthen our souls for all the conflict with temptation and evil which is appointed to all who follow Thee.

4. Divine Teacher, may we learn the lesson of Thy fast, that man shall not live by bread alone, but by every word that proceedeth out of the mouth of God.

5. Son of Man, tempted in all points like as we are, help us also to despise the glory of the kingdoms of this world, that we may serve only the Lord our God.

6. Almighty God, who commandedst the light to shine out of darkness, shine in our hearts to give the light of the knowledge of the glory of God in the face of our tempted and triumphant Lord.

(iv) By Thine Agony and Bloody Sweat, Good Lord, deliver us.

1. Lord Jesus, we desire to journey with Thee on the road to Jerusalem, that we may know more of the infinite love which carried Thee onwards in unfaltering steps until the Baptism of suffering, which Thou hadst to endure, was accomplished.

2. Lover of Men, let us see into the heart of Infinite Pity inflamed with the passion for the redemption of man which, by the darkness of Thy way, consecrated a new and living way for us into the holiest.

3. Sinless Saviour, help us to measure the greatness of our sin and the depth of our

ingratitude by Thy sufferings in the Garden of Gethsemane, the sinless Son of Man.

4. O Christ in agony, asking for the sympathy of Thy friends and disciples in that dread hour, let us not fail Thee in like manner, but may we ever be ready to suffer with and for our Lord.

5. Divine Victim, betrayed by those nearest to Thee, make us faithful in the least as well as the greatest things of life, that we may not increase the sorrows of the Crucified by our faithlessness.

6. Almighty God, who commandedst the light to shine out of darkness, shine in our hearts to give the light of the knowledge of the glory of God in the face of the suffering Christ of Gethsemane.

(v) BY THY CROSS AND PASSION,
     GOOD LORD, DELIVER US.

1. Man of Sorrows, help us to follow Thee along the Sorrowful Way, that we may learn the greatness of Thy shame and humiliation for our sake.

2. Divine Crossbearer, burdened with the sins of mankind, forgive us our share in that heavy burden.

3. O Christ, the chosen of God, Who wouldst not save Thyself, but in the hour of Thy Passion openedst up Paradise to the penitent Thief, grant

us before the Cross a like penitence, that with him we may enter into life eternal.

4. O Heart of Jesus, cleft for us, let the water and the blood flowing from Thy wounded side cleanse us from sin and make us worthy followers of the Crucified.

5. Divine Wayfarer, whose feet have carried Thee ever on errands of mercy and are now nailed to the shameful tree, Whose hands have ever lessened suffering, but are now pierced for us, help us before the Cross to consecrate all our goings and all our works to Thee.

6. Almighty God, Who commandedst the light to shine out of darkness, shine in our hearts to give the light of the knowledge of the glory of God in the face of the Crucified Christ.

(vi) By Thy Precious Death and Burial,
Good Lord, deliver us.

1. O Lord, help us, as we behold Thee in the tomb of Joseph of Arimathea, to understand the full extent of Thy obedience unto death, even the death of the Cross.

2. Son of Mary, grant that every broken-hearted mother, standing before the tomb of loved ones, may hear the voice which spake from the Cross, saying to the beloved disciple: "Son, behold thy Mother," and may find in that memory

the comfort and consolation which came to the Mother of Sorrows.

3. Divine Word, Creator of all things, teach us the meaning of the darkened sun and moon and stars, when all creation shuddered at Thy sufferings, the dying Son of God.

4. Sacred Victim, final and complete sacrifice, Thyself the great High Priest, make plain to us the boundless grace of the Heavenly Father revealed in the death of the Cross.

5. Head of the Church against which the gates of Hell cannot prevail, help us to pass onwards from the helplessness of the grave in the confidence that Thou art the Conqueror of death, and that the gates of hell shall not prevail against Thee, who art the Christ who died for us.

6. Almighty God, Who commandedst the light to shine out of darkness, shine in our hearts to give the light of the knowledge of the glory of God in the face of Thy Son obedient unto death.

(vii) By Thy Glorious Resurrection and
Ascension,
Good Lord, deliver us.

1. Lord of Life, Thou art not the dead Christ, or we were of all men most miserable. Our tears are turned into joy as we remember Thy words: "After three days, I will rise again."

2. O Thou Who art the firstfruits of the Resurrection, the grave could not hold Thee; the seals are broken; Thou are not here in the tomb, and with glad hearts we say: "O death, where is thy sting? O grave, where is thy victory?"

3. All hail, risen Christ! We glory in Thy triumph over death and the grave, and say: "Thanks be to God Who giveth us the victory through our Lord Jesus Christ."

4. All-conquering Christ, Thine enemies are put under Thy feet. Thy reign is established, for the last enemy to be destroyed is death. In Thy triumph we mortals of yesterday can face death, the last enemy, rejoicing in the final and complete victory of our Lord and Saviour Jesus Christ.

5. Ascended Lord, fulfil in us the last promise of Olivet and send upon us, we beseech Thee, the power of the Holy Spirit, that we may be witnesses to all men of Thy power, the Crucified, to lead captivity captive, and to receive gifts for men, and to give to men life in abundance.

6. Almighty God Who commandedst the light to shine out of darkness, shine in our hearts to give the light of the knowledge of the glory of God in the face of our Risen and Ascended Lord.

A Meditation before receiving the Holy Communion

1. Almighty God, who hast so loved us as to give Thine only Son to die for us, increase our faith in Him, as we obey His commands and approach the Table of His love.

2. O Lord Jesus Christ, deepen at this time our sorrow for our sins, as we confess that with Peter we have often denied Thee, and with Judas we have sold Thee.

3. Spirit Divine, attend our prayers, and so cleanse our hearts that we may worthily receive our Lord.

4. Thou, O blessed Lord Jesus, has taught us that Thy Flesh is meat indeed, and Thy Blood is drink indeed, and that whoso eateth Thy Flesh and drinketh Thy Blood dwelleth in Thee and Thou in him. Help us to examine and prove ourselves that we may worthily commemorate the gift of Thyself to be our Life.

5. Thou invitest us to come not only into the Presence of God, but unto the Table of the Lord, and to be one of the guests of the Lord of all the

world; may the greatness of this privilege enable us to put away all thoughts of the business and of the joys and of the cares of earth.

6. Since we are but beggars who, nevertheless, are invited to sup with a King, we can only humble ourselves and give thanks, praying for the grace of devotion, for we have need of Thee, and not Thou of us. Refresh us with heavenly food, cover our nakedness with Thy grace, inflame our coldness with the fire of Thy love, and help us to despise all earthly things in the presence of the King of Kings.

7. In this holy fellowship may we come with joy and gratitude unto Mount Sion, the City of the Living God, the Heavenly Jerusalem, to innumerable hosts of Angels, to the general assembly and Church of the first-born, unto the spirits of just men made perfect, and to Jesus the Mediator of the New Covenant and to the blood of sprinkling that speaketh better things than that of Abel.

8. As we join in communion with Thee and with Thy Saints on earth and with all the glorious company who are before Thy Throne in Heaven, may we know indeed the power of unity by which we are brought into oneness with Thee and become Members of Thee, living branches of the True Vine.

9. May our souls be cleansed by Thy Precious Blood, and our sins swallowed up in the abyss of

Thy Mercy and our iniquities consumed in the fire of Thy Love.

10. At this festival of the Divine Love may we renounce all love of self, that the reign of Thy Love may be established in our hearts.

11. Before Thy Cross may we hate all the sins that have nailed Thee to the Tree, and abhor them, and be filled with the sorrow and contrition of Thine Apostle Peter and of Mary Magdalene and of all to whom the Cross has made plain the blackness of their sin and the wonder of Thy forgiving Love.

12. On this Altar do Thou take possession of our hearts and receive from us the homage which we owe to Thee as our sovereign Lord, that hereafter we may serve Thee in newness of life, to the honour and glory of Thy Name, through Jesus Christ, our Lord.

A Meditation During Holy Communion

"SOUL OF CHRIST, SANCTIFY ME !"

1. May the passion of sacrifice, the passion of humility, and the passion of love that carried Thee forward through Gethsemane to Calvary, cleanse our hearts that we may perfectly love Thee and comprehend with all the saints the fulness of Thy love for a sinning world, and Thy purpose to redeem mankind from sin.

"BODY OF CHRIST, SAVE ME!"

2. Since it was to redeem us from our sin that Thou didst take upon Thee the body of our humiliation, and subject Thyself to all the trials and temptations of our mortal life, may the object of Thine Incarnation be fulfilled in our lives at this time, as we contemplate the love that brought Thee down to earth to suffer for us men and for our salvation, and to give that sacred Body to be nailed to the Tree.

"BLOOD OF CHRIST, INEBRIATE ME!"

3. Thou hast taught us, Blessed Master, to abide in Thee as the branch abides in the vine, that we may be quickened into fruit-bearing by Thy Blood, and we pray that, as the branch is made fruitful by the sap of the vine, this day as we receive the Wine which Thou dost give us, saying, "This is My Blood of the New Testament," we may be quickened thereby to a new consecration which none can understand save those who love Thee.

"WATER FROM THE SIDE OF CHRIST, WASH ME!"

4.   "Let the water and the blood
From Thy riven side which flowed
Be of sin the double cure,
Cleanse me from its guilt and power."

"PASSION OF CHRIST, STRENGTHEN ME!"

5. May the thought of all that Thou didst suffer in that shameful and bitter death, urge, inflame and drive us to love Thee more than we have ever done, and strengthen us to devote and give all our life and our labour and our love to Thee.

"O GOOD JESU! HEAR ME!"

6. With Thy beloved Disciple, we lift up our eyes to Thee, hanging upon the Cross, and we pray

that as Thou didst hear him and give him his special call to service, so now there may come to us from Thee some message that we may hear and understand and obey.

"WITHIN THY WOUNDS HIDE ME!"

7. O wounded Heart of pity and of love, cleft for me, let me hide myself in Thee; O pierced hands, embrace me now and always, and keep me from falling.

"SUFFER ME NOT TO BE SEPARATED FROM THEE!"

8. I would stay here at the foot of the Cross, but Thy service and my duty drive me forth again. Go with me, Blessed Master, let me never be separated from Thee, may every hour be filled with Thy Presence.

"FROM THE MALICIOUS ENEMY DEFEND ME!"

9. The Cross tells me how strong is the hatred of the Evil One for my Lord and Master, and how keen is the malice of sinful men as they contemplate Thy perfection. The servant is not greater than his master; the enemy encompasses my soul to destroy it; let me abide ever in the secret place, O Crucified Master.

"IN THE HOUR OF MY DEATH, CALL ME! AND BID
ME COME TO THEE, THAT WITH THY SAINTS I MAY
PRAISE THEE, FOR EVER AND EVER."

10. In this Holy Communion, Blessed Lord,
Thou hast given me a foretaste of the fellowship
with Thee, and with the innumerable company
who are before Thy Throne in Heaven. Deepen
and strengthen that fellowship until the river of
death is passed, and Thou dost call me to that City
of which Thou art the light and the joy; where,
through all Eternity, I may realise, more and more
fully, the love that loved unto death.

A Meditation after Communion

1. Bless the Lord, O my soul, and forget not all His benefits; for He hath regarded the lowliness of His servant. He that is mighty hath magnified me, and holy is His Name. He hath filled the hungry with good things, and hath remembered His mercy as He promised to our forefathers.

2. Let my soul, O Lord, be filled with the joy of Thy Presence, as I taste how gracious Thou art. Henceforth be Thou the joy of my heart and my portion for ever.

3. O Great Physician, by Thy stripes my sickness is healed. With joyful haste Thou camest from Heaven to save me. Let Thy purpose be fulfilled in my whole being, body, soul and spirit.

4. Thou Good Shepherd, Who hast given Thy life for the sheep, let me henceforth lack nothing in the green pastures wherein Thou now feedest me, until I come to the pastures of eternity, to be sustained for ever by the food of angels in communion and fellowship with Thee, my glorified and triumphant Master and Lord.

5. Thou true Light of the world, Who enlightenest every man that cometh into the world,

who art the only light of the Eternal City, let Thy Presence illumine my path this day and always.

6. King of Heaven and Earth, Who hast welcomed me to sup with Thee this day, accept my humble praise for all the treasures of Thy love, and let my soul rejoice continually in the immeasurable riches of Thy bounty.

7. Thou who art my love and my joy, may I die unto the world for love of Thee, Who for love of me hast died upon the Cross.

8. Lamb of God that takest away the sins of the world, let not my sins ever again crucify the Son of God, the Lord of Life, but redeem my soul from the power of the Evil One, henceforth and for ever.

9. Thou Who art the portion of mine inheritance and of my cup, take for Thine own every power of my soul, my memory, my mind, my will; all is Thine, bought with the price of Thine own life blood.

10. Father of all mercies, and God of all grace, Thou hast done great things for me to-day, whereof my soul rejoices. Here and now, stirred by these tokens of the love of my Lord, I surrender my life, my all, to Thee, henceforth to be governed by Thy sovereign will; keep all in Thy care, henceforth and for ever, my King and my Lord.

A Meditation on Our Apostolate

The following passages are suggested for free meditation. The more they are used in this way and the following outline left behind, the more will the purpose of this outline be accomplished.

St. Matthew xxviii, *verses* 16–20.
St. Mark xvi, *verse* 20.
St. Luke xxiv.
Acts i, *verses* 1–11.

1. Almighty God, Who in times past hast spoken to the Fathers by the Prophets, we praise Thee that in these last days Thou hast spoken to us by Thy Son, Whom Thou hast appointed Heir of all things.

2. O Lord Jesus, we desire now to journey in company and fellowship with Thee and with Thy disciples to Bethany, and to share in the blessing which Thou, the risen Christ, dost bestow upon those who walk with Thee by the way.

3. We would stand with Thee upon the Mount of Olives, and hear Thy gracious words of comfort, consolation and commission to Thy disciples, as

Thou didst call them from discipleship to apostleship, from being learners in the school of the Galilæan Lake to become the teachers of the world.

4. As we worship Thee, the risen Saviour, confirm our faith and quicken our love, and as some of Thy disciples at Bethany were troubled with doubts, so in the weakness of our faith we ask for such a revelation of Thy love and Thy power as shall dispel all our unbelief and fill us with that confidence in Thee and Thy mission which shall make our lives fruitful to Thy honour and glory.

5. With Thy disciples we worship Thee, the risen Saviour, in penitence for our denials, which we have shared with Peter, our unbelief which we have shared with Thomas, and our failures when we have forsaken Thee in times of special trial. We therefore pray that Thou wilt now confirm our faith and quicken our love, and dispel all doubt and misgiving by the revelation of Thy power. Give us a great confidence in Thee and our own mission, which shall make our lives fruitful to Thy honour and glory.

6. Since the Father hath given Thee all authority we ask in like manner that by that authority Thou wilt commission us to carry on Thy work in the world.

7. The nations of old did not need Thee more than do the multitudes of India and China and

the isles of the sea. The wrath of man still grievously afflicts those who are faithful to Thee even in many lands which bear Thy name. As we view these things from Olivet, may the call to an apostolate be deepened and quickened in our lives.

8. May we hear Thy voice in our hearts saying, "As my Father hath sent Me, even so send I you." May we declare freedom to those who are the slaves of sin: may we open the prison doors of ignorance and folly to the wisdom that comes from Thee, and may the song of the angels of peace on earth amongst men of goodwill be our message to the nations who are still bound by the fetters of hatred. Send us forth, we beseech Thee, to seek Thy kingdom, which is not of this world, and which comes down from God out of Heaven. May the promise of Pentecost which Thou gavest to Thy disciples, help us to proclaim a kingdom, not of might nor of worldly power, not of force nor of worldly wisdom, but of the Spirit of God. Thus may it be ours to come to the City of God whose twelve gates are open day and night that all nations may enter.

A Meditation on the Lord's Prayer

1. Let us commence our meditation with the petition of the Disciples, "Lord, teach us to pray."

Let us picture in our minds the occasion when these words were first used, and contrast this scene with the giving of the Law, and the changed relation to God which is revealed.

Let us rejoice that we have the same wonderful Teacher as the Disciples—All-wise, Gracious and Loving, and ask that His gift of the Holy Spirit may help our infirmities as we seek to understand all that His words should convey.

"OUR FATHER WHICH ART IN HEAVEN"

2. Almighty God, we praise Thee for the revelation of Thy Son Jesus Christ, in Whom dwelleth all the fulness of the Godhead bodily, and Who is the first-born among many brethren, and we rejoice that He has taught us when we pray to address Thee as "Our Father."

We rejoice that we can never be orphaned and never be alone, because the Everlasting God is our Father.

Thou, O God, art omnipresent, omnipotent, omniscient, and yet we can claim Thee as our Father.

We adore Thee as our Heavenly Father, Who dost

from Thy throne behold all the dwellers upon earth, Who nevertheless art revealed to us by Christ as our Father.

We beseech Thee to reveal to all Thy separated children their unity in Thee, their Heavenly Father, and to end all the unhappy divisions in Thy family upon earth.

"HALLOWED BE THY NAME"

3. We thank Thee, O God, that Thou art revealed to us in One whose "Name shall be called Wonderful, Counsellor, Mighty God, Everlasting Father, Prince of Peace" and that "of the increase of His government and Peace there shall be no end."

We recall the reverence with which the Jewish nation treated Thy name, O Lord Jehovah.

We confess with shame and confusion of face that our lives have too often lessened the honour and respect that men have paid to Thy Name.

We pray that at all times we may remember that the name we bear was given us "in the name of the Father, and the Son and the Holy Spirit."

"THY KINGDOM COME"

4. We confess that we have not obeyed Thy Son's injunction to place first and foremost, in all things, the coming of Thy Kingdom.

We mourn that there is so much that contradicts Thy rule in our country, in our Church, in our homes, and in our own lives.

"THY WILL BE DONE ON EARTH AS IT IS IN HEAVEN"

5. Give us, we beseech Thee, to realise in how many ways we have thwarted Thy Will, and thereby delayed the coming of Thy Kingdom.

Help us to take the standard of Heaven for the measure of earth, and to contrast the perfect obedience of those who "are before the Throne of God, and serve Him day and night in His Temple," with the contradiction of Thy purposes all around us and within us.

Help us to consider how far we can amend these things, and bring the peace and joy and love of Heaven into the life of earth, and change earth's discord into the complete harmony of the song of the Redeemed.

"AND GIVE US THIS DAY OUR DAILY BREAD"

6. We ask for ourselves what we need for this day of the bread that perisheth.

We also pray that we may feed upon Christ by faith in our hearts, since He is our Heavenly Food.

We here recall our Lord's words, "My Flesh is meat indeed, and My Blood is drink indeed; he that eateth My Flesh and drinketh My Blood dwelleth in Me and I in him."

We pray, O Lord, for all those who lack the daily bread for their bodies, and still more for those who have never learned to feed upon Thee by faith in their hearts.

"FORGIVE US OUR TRESPASSES"

7. We confess all the sins that we have done against Thy commands, transgressing Thy Will and preventing Thy purpose since last we knelt before Thee.

"AS WE FORGIVE THEM THAT TRESPASS AGAINST US"

Help us, O God to forgive all who have in any way wronged us, and so to do because we hope to be forgiven.

Grant, we beseech Thee, O Lord, that all whom we have wronged may be healed, and may forgive us.

"LEAD US NOT INTO TEMPTATION"

8. We thank Thee, O God, for Thine assurance that we shall never be tempted above that we are able to bear, and Thou wilt provide a way of escape from every temptation, that we may be able to bear it, and we pray for grace and wisdom to take the open way.

"AND DELIVER US FROM EVIL"

9. Finally we pray for deliverance from the Evil One, and ascribe all dominion and honour to Him, who with the Son and the Holy Spirit reigns, God over all, for ever and ever. Amen.

APPENDIX

*A Pilgrim's Chapbook

THE PATTERN OF THE MASTER

ARRANGED BY

THE REV. GILBERT SHAW, M.A.

Organising Secretary of the Association for Promoting Retreats

" For Thy Life is our way, and in it we walk to Thee Who art our crown by holy patience " (*Imitation* III. xviii. 3).

———

It has been impressed on the compiler of this series, that many people would be helped to pray better if they were provided with devotions and instructions on less formal and stereotyped lines than is usual, and published at a price that all can afford. It is to meet this need that these booklets have been prepared. They take their name from one of the Missionary Training Colleges, which has been sending men out to the mission-field for nearly fifty years, and to whose students, past and present, the series is dedicated.

The compiler hopes that the new shape of booklet adopted will meet the difficulties of those who complained that the old numbers were awkward to use; but he would remind them that one of the objects of the series is cheapness, and that much has to be sacrificed to that.

He would also, as before, acknowledge his debt to the devotional writers of the past, and would ask to be forgiven if he has unconsciously made use of phrases made familiar by modern authors, and so fallen into any unintentional plagiarism.

---

* The following pages are extracted from Part II of "A Pilgrim's Chapbook" published at 6d. by Messrs. A. R. Mowbray & Co. Ltd., 28, Margaret Street, London, W.1. I am greatly indebted to the generosity of the Reverend Gilbert Shaw for allowing me to publish this.

𝔄 𝔓ilgrim's 𝔠hapbook

INTRODUCTION.

"No one can attain divine exaltation or singular sweetness except by passing through the image of my human abasement and bitterness" (*Blessed Suso, "Eternal Wisdom"*).

Our life in Christ is an achievement as well as a gift. It is by the renewing of our minds by co-operation with grace that we walk or progress towards Him as well as in Him.

The way is certain for He is the Way, but we must walk His way and not our way. He calls us to copy His very way of life: "Learn of Me, for I am meek and lowly in heart." Humility is the first virtue of our renewed life, in which the old Adam is brought to nothing that Christ may reign in us through detachment from all creatures and by poverty of self. Entering into our own nothingness we may find peace for our souls, in finding our true outgoing in love, in purity that we may be with Him and see Him, by courage that would keep us close to Him whatever may be the cost in effort and suffering.

Humility, Detachment, Poverty, Love, Purity, Courage: six words describing the saintly character, as Evelyn Underhill says.

If we would achieve such a character, growing in grace by grace, the words must not only be words to us, but possessions lived for, and with, until our whole life is marked and conditioned by their acquisition.

The exercises here set out have been arranged under the heading of these words with a general introduction to be used before each based on the submission of each part of our nature to God's guidance. We possess understanding, affections, and will, and each one must play its part in making the offering to God—each part must share in the labour of achievement.

Intellect alone is sterile; and affection, unregulated by intellect, purposeless, and, without will, only a desire and impotent; while will, without intellect and affection, is without point or object.

However, if the understanding or intellect does not want to meditate, but only to rest content on one consideration, let it do so. It is active, and is giving its strength to the affections directing all the emotional life to one point. If affection seems to fail and feels no taste, do not be anxious, but support the whole attention by the will; the less is known or felt, the less of self; the harder, drier, more toilsome is the way, the closer must the will cling to Him; through fire and water He must lead us till we come to the wealthy place of His delights.

PREPARATION.

"The soul that finds no pleasure out of God cannot be long unvisited by the Beloved."

—*St. John of the Cross.*

O God, Thou didst make me.

O God, Thou hast redeemed me.

O God, Thou helpest me.

Without Thee I am nothing, less than nothing,
    a rebel to Thy love,
    a despiser of Thy grace.

O God, have pity upon me a sinner;
grant me a new vision of Thy love
    and of Thy will for me.

Give me stillness in my soul that I may know
    Thee and love Thee, and grant me strength to
    do Thy will,

O God, my all.

O God, Thou hast given bread for my body, and
    silence for my soul.

How can my body live without bread, how can my
    soul live without silence?

O ocean of Love, stillness profound, light and life of
    all who come to Thee, draw me into Thy still
    peace, that all the noise of things be stilled and
    the music of my soul be all one note, Thyself
    alone, my God, my all.

O God, I am Thine;
  move Thou my prayer, that I may seek Thee:
O God, I am Thine;
  stir Thou my heart, that I may find Thee:
O God, I am Thine;
  enslave my will, that I may hold to Thee:
  enfold me in Thyself, that all my being be to
    Thee alone.
        My God, my all.

O God, Thou art my God;
  move Thou each separate power of my being,
    that all its occupation be of Thee.
Cleanse Thou my memory, that it may only keep
    the impress of Thy love.
Make quick my intellect, that every active thought
    may turn to Thee.
Support my will, that all I do may be for Thee,
  joyfully accepting all things in Thee, for Thee,
    through Thee,
        O God, my all.

Father, I, the prodigal, do turn to Thee; seek Thou
    me out upon the road, that all my thought and
    mind be filled with Thee, and I may find, and,
    finding, love.
Incarnate Love, that died for me, inflame my weak
    affections; that burning in Thy purest flame of
    love, all that is not Thine may be consumed
    and purged away, that so I may truly love.

Thou Comforter and Guide, move Thou my will,
    that, one in love with Thee, I may in love
    increase.

O Blessed Trinity, that art the source of all my
    being, grant me such love that, dying to myself
    I may return Thy love, and so Thou mayest be
    my only end, my God, my all.

O God, my Love,
    from Thee I come,
    Thine I am,
    to Thee I go,

O God, Thou Mystery of ever-loving love, from
    Love, to Love, in Love,
    O ever-loving God of Love.

O God, Thou hast made us for Thyself, that we
    might be the mirror of Thy loveliness:
    Thou hast taken our life to be Thine own, that
    we may see Thy beauty as Thou wouldst have
    it be in human form.

O Jesu, God and Man, so draw us to Thyself, that
    lost in Thee we may find life.

Jesus,
    Crown of virtue, perfect pattern of the human
        good,
    in Thy humility we see the Way Thou willest
        every human soul to go.

Give us the grace to follow Thee, that learning of
Thy meek and lowly heart we may find rest,
the rest of love,
stillness of an everlasting energy,
self lost in giving love and love's return.

Jesus,
Light of the Eternal Brightness,
Fire of the Everlasting Love,
Thy awful Purity declares the Truth;
help us to die, that by detachment freed from all
except the Father's will we may for ever burn
one flame with Thee.

Jesus,
Fountain of Life,
Friend, Comrade, King,
Who holdest out to us the chalice of Thyself,
teach us to feel the beating of Thy sacred Heart,
that we alive in Thee may know
our life is dying and our rest is suffering,
our riches poverty, our poverty abundant
wealth.

My King, my Love, my only Hope, my Jesus, Thy
life is all too clear for those who read, too hard,
too high:
grant me Thy courage that I may share Thy pain.
O Love, Who dost awaken souls to journey forth in
faith,

leading Thy people through the wilderness,
    guiding the feet of them that seek through
    fire and water so that they may reach the
    wealthy place of Thy surpassing love:
grant me Thy awaking touch and guidance all
    the way.

Jesus, Who dost call Thy servants out of the world,
    that they may live within Thy heart, the very
    members of Thy Body, triumphant but yet
    crucified;
    too high, too hard the Way, unless, Lord Jesus,
    Thou art mine.

HUMILITY

"Through this virtue more than anything else,
all saints were and are men according to God's
heart. In short, in this virtue the whole discipline
of Christian wisdom consisteth." (*Blosius, "Sanctuary of the Faithful Soul."*)

Learn of Me, my Saviour says, to rate thyself the
    servant of all living, to hold within thy heart
    no thought but that the Father may be
    glorified, and so find rest, and life and healing
    for thy soul.
Woe is me, I am undone; before Thy Way, Thy
    Truth, Thy Life, my self-complacency, my
    pride, my indolence, is ever more and more
    revealed.

Touch Thou my lips with Thy burning fire, burn
    Thou my dross, grant me contrition that all
    my days be lived in penitential lowliness.

Jesus, Thou the uncreated whole in what was
    Thine in all eternity, whole in all our human
    nature, True God, True Man, in all the pleni-
    tude of meekness taking the form of a servant,
    being made in the likeness of men,
O Love, divine from all eternity,
O Love, most truly human from the moment of Thy
    Incarnation,
    grant us the grace to worship Thee, adoring Thy
    humility, loving Thee, our Saviour and our
    friend.

Jesus, by Whom the worlds were made, Light out
    of Light of the Eternal Majesty, for Thee there
    was no room in the inn.
    Without the gate, shut out from all Thy world of
    men, in nature's stillest hour, Thy hid divinity
    was first acclaimed by Mary's love and Joseph's
    awe.
    The cattle's manger cradled Thee a helpless babe;
    no courtiers to proclaim Thy worth, but
    humble shepherds and the old wise men;
    No tribute but the symbol gifts to declare the
    truth of Kingship, the life of Deity, the way of
    sacrifice.

My God, so comest Thou to every heart, hid from
the pomp of earth, the pride of life, the lustful
eye.

The house of prayer that should have welcomed
Thee, Thy rebellious children made a den of
thieves, a place of beasts and marketing and
strife.

And I—how often have I turned Thee from the
door by pride, intolerance or fear, by greed and
avarice.

And I—when Thou didst live Thy life so poor and
meek to win my love,—
my life has been all comfort, ease, enjoyment,
and for praise and acclamation ever I have
sought.

Thou wast subject to Joseph and Thy blessed
Mother,
and all Thy life was to obey the Father's will;
and mine one long rebellion seeking self,
one long misuse of all Thy grace.

Awake, my soul, to follow all the way;
the crowded inn, the noise and tumult of the
world,
refused Thee birth.

Take Thou my heart and enter in and drive without
the passions and the world; guide Thou my

worship and prepare a place where Thou mayest dwell, Thy life my way; let nothing of my own make void Thy work, my God, my all.

DETACHMENT

"He who aims at the attainment of God's love must needs confine all his heart, mind, and energy for that single aim" (*St. Francis de Sales* "*The Love of God,*" xii. 3).

My God, my all,

Draw Thou my eyes from all but Thee lest they behold vanity; and quicken Thou me in Thy way.

All things created are but vanity unless they form the footsteps to Thy Throne.

My very soul is worse to me than any devil because it comes between me and my God.

Grant me that vision of myself without which my soul may never know Thee. My God, my all.

Grant me such light that each recess and corner of my soul may be illumined, and grant the resolution that will fear no pain, but grasp each wayward action and all that is not sanctified for Thee, that Thou mayest take it thence.

Teach me to be alone with Thee.

O God, why do I fear to be alone?
My treasure is all dissipated among the things of
earth, I crave for comfort from my fellow
creatures, my interest is in the things that
perish, my life is lukewarm, and sorrowfully
I turn away when Thou commandest me to
follow Thee alone.

O Lord, forgive. Let nothing hold my heart but
only Thee,

O soul, look well upon thy life.
What dost thou possess?
What canst thou do without?
What things are idols yet with thee?

Let nothing be possessed for its own sake or merit,
for even the harmless doves in man-made cages
Thou didst bid forth from Thy Father's house.

O loving Saviour, Who dost bid me leave all else
but to endure Thy cross and fellowship, grant
me to follow Thee, Thyself all stripped and
emptied, all for love of me, myself all naked
of all save Thee; clothe me with Thy detachment from all save only Thee.
The Father's will be done in me, as done in Thee.
Grant me to know Thee, O my Love;
to find in Thee the suffering of Thy fellowship,
the rest of Love, self lost in giving love and
love's return.

Help me to die with Thee, that I may for ever burn one flame with Thee.   O God, my Love.

POVERTY

"He hath dispersed abroad and given to the poor; yes, He hath dispersed to many persons, He gave, He did not sell; it was to the poor, too, not to the rich" (*The last words of St. Gilbert of Sempringham*).

Possessing nothing, yet making many rich, thorn-crowned and reigning from the Tree, Love's wealth was bleeding wounds, stripes whence healing flows, a broken heart, an ever-springing fount of Love that knows no end nor yet beginning, the Heart of God made manifest in human flesh declaring all the riches of Thine everlasting love.

Grant me, O Love, a share of this Thy wealth, that having nothing of my own I may possess the virtue of Thy wounds, my sins' forgiveness and in Thy Heart the offerings of my pain.

Thy riches no human wealth or toil may buy, freely Thou givest to those who will accept nor count the cost of harbouring Thy wealth of cross and shame that they may share Thy joy.

Look well, O soul, within thy treasury.

Each thought and motive weigh, that no idol of
thyself or of the world may claim thy heart, so
that thy love may be His love, and so, returned
in Love's own usury, the talents of thy soul
may find fruition and increase according to
the increase of His gifts.

It is the empty soul that learns the hunger of great
love, even as the parched land in agony of
dumbness waits the recreating rain by which
the desert blossoms as the rose and all the
plain is filled with life's new melody.

A great cry to my Love is emptiness, the hunger-
ing and thirsting shall be satisfied.

Revive, O Lord, within my soul the spring of Life,
that from my nothingness may flow the living
waters of Thy peace—the Gospel that Thy
slave in Thee is free, free from all life's bitter
bondage, the cares and tumults, selfishness and
fierce idolatries that like ill weeds grow up and
choke the grain Thou sowest in the field.

Thy Life the seed, my soul the ground.

Look well, O soul, art thou a road, a common
haunt of other folk, a way wherein there is no
rest but idle chatter of the crowd?

Hast thou dug deep and cleared the soil of all
that lies beneath the outward semblance of
thy life?

O soul, if thou wouldst be the ground wherein
the Word may grow to fill thy life, it was within the stable He was born, the workshop knew
His growing days, and the perfect wheat was
manifest in death.

Except a soul shall die it cannot live. Be nothing,
O my soul, have one desire to be *by* Jesus led,
with Jesus on the way, that *in* Jesus all shall
be a life of dying, and a rest of suffering,
thy riches poverty and poverty abundant
wealth.

Too high, too hard this way
unless, my Jesus, Thou art mine.

LOVE

"Love will tend upwards and is not to be de-
tained by things on earth." (*Imitation*, III, v.).

Who may sing the song of Love?
Those only who give all, without reserve, hold
nothing back,
'tis they who know the joy, the quickening
pain of Love;
'tis they who taught by adoration hold the
Heart of Love,
and touch all loveless hearts to life by giving
Love.

From Love in Love the leaping flame of Love is
    spread, for none can love except by Love
    possessed.
  The love that is outpoured was first Love's gift
    of Love.
  Give, give, and give again
    is Love's own song.
  For Love is giving love and there is no end to
    Love.
  Love is as the incense which giveth up its sweet-
    ness as it is consumed.

Naked of all save love went Love, till naked in
    body, wounded, pierced in agony of love,
  Love broke the casket of the fount of love, that
    He might draw all souls to find their end within
    the Heart of God.

Love waits so still,
    for love must answer Love,
    and we have wounded Love, betrayed, denied
    our Love.

Silent upon the Tree, made sin for us, Love waits
    that by the utmost gift of love, His broken
    Heart of Love, sin might no longer have
    dominion over us.

O loving Lord, Thine eyes looked lovingly upon
    that woman in the hall, and at Thy feet she
    wept in answering love.

Thine eyes searched Peter's face when Thou
 wast ringed with scorn and enemies, and he
 went out and wept most bitterly in loving
 grief.

Upon the Cross in desolation's hour Thy quiet gaze
 did draw the thief,
 O Lord, remember me.

I have ringed Thee round with hostility, denied
 Thee,
 I have sinned as rebel misusing all the gifts of
 life and love Thou gavest me.
 I have sinned by failing to respond to all Thy
 perfect will for me.
 Lord, give me love that I may know true
 penitence.

Lord, give me such desire for Thyself alone:
 That I may hate myself,
 the self that wounds, scourges, nails and crucifies
 Thee still,
 That I may take each several power of my
 life and crucify the natural part of me, that
 all may be renewed, held fast in love.

Three nails may hold me fast to Thee—
 obedience, dependence, reparation.
 Never to seek myself, but only walk love's way.
 Casting away all else, love only to possess, and
 with love to share Love's giving of His love.

Prostrate before the feet of Love, Love's broken
   feet,
   two ways alone of Life appear—
      to crucify Him, or with Him be crucified.

Love's only song is giving, giving all.

How calm, majestically He walks life's paths;
   How sweetly calls His friends to come apart into
      the desert place: "Be still and know," look
      out over God's harvest fields and pray.
   Calm amid the storm He sleeps,

Love's power is of stillness born.

The fire of Love Divine is still.
   No flickering flame, the living movement of ever
      rendered love.
   Hid deep within the mystery of the Unity in
      Three, it burns a living darkness that is light,
      and light so bright that darkness is its flame.

O God, Thou art the centre of my being, the
      homing place of all desire, the universe of all
      and every love.

My Jesus, Light and Love, Who showest me the
      inmost Heart of Love reigning upon the Tree,
      the sacred Heart, Whose death wound was the
      Gate of Life,
   My Jesus, take Thou Thy dart and spear of love,

Pierce Thou my heart that I may love, nor find
   a limit to my love.

Still, vibrant, giving, agonising, is the soul of Love;
   its fruit more love, more pain, more longing,
   more desire, more souls for God, more sorrow,
   deeper penitence, a cry in all the world that
   Thou, O God, art Love; an anguish that man's
   freedom turns from God; more souls, O God,
   more souls to love Thee every day,
      O Love, O God of Love.

PURITY

"For as long as He findeth not His image reformed in thee, He is strange and far from thee"
(*Hilton, "Scale of Perfection," chapter* 1).

The pure in heart, the single eye, alone shall see
   my God.
O God, Thy Majesty abides so still, so far apart
   from my self-filled and wayward life.
O radiant Purity, that lives one fire, the fire of
   Love, consume me quite within Thy quench-
   less flame.
Thou virgin-born, Thy life, the Purity of God on
   earth in human frame, may we possess Thy
   love in purity, not for Thy gifts or favours but
   for Thyself alone, our all and every thought
   and wish and will Thine everlasting glory.

My Lord, my King, how awful is Thy Presence in the sacramental veils, the Purity of God surrendered into human hands and human guardianship.

How dreadful is the place, where on Thy countless thrones faith hails Thee present, or in dim unknowing is Thy Majesty revered.

How clean the heart should be that welcomes Thee its King, how pure the living house of prayer wherein Thou wouldst abide.

How wonderfully Thou didst form that nothing but Thyself may satisfy my soul's most inward longing.

My life is Thine. Each day be then a gift to give to Thee; a life to live for Thee, to live Thy Life, for Thou didst give it me, my life is Thine.

O Love, to Thee I do resign myself,
   let nothing of my wretched self remain but all of Thee.

I do resign myself to bear whatever Thou dost send to bear and to rejoice.

For love of Thee, and in conformity to Thy good will, I now resign myself if ever it may be Thy will.

To suffer shame and slander, unearned rebuke, to be forgotten of my friends, to want for food and natural comfort, to be abandoned and ignored by all my fellow men, so that I may have none to hold to but only Thee my God.

To suffer sickness and infirmity, to die alone in a strange land and among strangers, to endure aridity and pain of soul, to follow Thee blindly, not seeking distraction or comfort in any creature, to be content to spend and to be spent for Thee.

Take, O Lord, my freedom and my choice of things.

O Lord, Thou gavest it to me that I might be freed from sin and all that hampers me returning Thy love, my love to Thee.

To Thee, O Lord, I do return Thy gifts; dispose of me according to Thy will.

Let nothing cloud the mirror of my soul, Thy face alone illumine it.

Let nothing share the altar of my heart, lest strange fire, born of my unruled desire, burn thereon and cause Thee to depart.

Burn Thou alone within the temple Thou didst fashion for Thyself, and burning burn all dross of self away, so that Thou mayest ever stay and never from my life depart, that in Thy Purity I may obtain, the veil of flesh being rent by Thee, my place before the Father's Throne hid in Thy Life within all Deity.

COURAGE

"Above all the graces and gifts of the Holy Spirit which Christ grants to His friends is that of self-conquest and willingly bearing sufferings, injuries, and reproaches and discomforts for the love of Christ " (*Little Flowers of St. Francis of Assisi*).

O Love, O Purity,
>How may I come to find eternal rest in Thee?
>How may I bring with me the souls Thou givest me to bring?

>The seed must perish that new life may spring.
>The wheat must die or ever it alone must stay.
>>O Jesus, Thou art our guide.
>>And in Thy life alone we have life,
>>Teach us to die that we may live.

>By the shadow of Thy Cross upon Thy cradle.
>By Thine infant acceptance of the myrrh.
>By the words that told of Thy decease upon the mountain top.
>By Thy face fast set toward Jerusalem.
>By Thy silence before Thine accusers.
>By the joyful acceptance of the Cross.
>By the awful stillness of Thine Incarnate Life unlifted before the world of men.

Pity our frailty.
Give us Thyself
>that, nestling in Thy broken Heart, we may endure with Thee the agony of sinful man's return to holiness.

O Jesu, by Thine awful penitence for us, bring us
safely through those cleansing fires of Love,
when hope seems dead and love can find no
answer to its love, and faith is blind obedience
bearing agony and Thou art not, and all is sin
and shame and loss and nothing is, but horror
of myself, and of the world and of the power of
the air.

O God, in the hour of desolation grant us the faith
to know that Thine absence from our consciousness is all our loss, nor doubt that in the
darkness Thou art near.

Immortal Love, in man delivering man, lead on
Thy servant by Thy way from death to life.
Set Thou so clear before our eyes Thy way of
conquest that I may never fear, but loving
ever will to share the cost.
Hold me so close that I may touch Thy wounds and
feel the beating of Thy Heart—
The very wounds I gave Thee, O my Love,
The very Heart that broke for me,
The very wounds that conquered me and set me
free so I might love Thee, O my Love,
The very Heart that desolated poured its love to
draw me in.

O Love, Thy might is pain and desolation,
Thy victory humiliation and life's outpouring,

O God, how sweet it is to serve Thee in darkness
and unknowing, in contradiction and all undone, forlorn, bereft, alone.

'Tis Faith that cleaves the darkness like a sword
and cleaving pierces him who wields.
'Tis Hope that never can be satisfied till Love's
most perfect rest shall dawn.
'Tis Love that here can know no rest, while sin and
evil still Christ's Body crucify.

The strength of Love is faith,
the agony of Love is hope.
O soul, be strong, be agonised, one life thou hast on
earth by which to give more love and yet more
love to Him Who lovest thee to such extremity.

Jesus, by Thy love for men,
grant us Thy servants strength that we may
love them too, so serving them we may serve
Thee and satisfy the hunger of Thy Heart.
O Love, if men did learn to love Thee,
then all the world would know Thy peace and
Thou wouldst reign in every heart.
O Love, reign Thou in mine that I may count no
cost, nor fear no pain.
Make Thou my hands and feet Thy very own,
my heart be broken of Thy pain,
complete Thy victory in this my soul
that love may draw more souls to Thee.

O Mystery of ever-loving Love, that love must give
    and love must share and never cease from
    loving toil, from Love in Love to Love, O
    loving God of Love.

CONCLUSION

"Therefore rest thee here, comfort thee here,
live in Christ's heart without end." (*A Meditation
of the Five Wounds of Jesus Christ by an Early
English writer.*)

Jesus, my Love, my King, my God, my friend, my
    life, my all, my only refuge and enduring hope,
    my Jesus.
To know Thee, O my Love, be all my aim,
    in Thee be lost, in Thee be found.
My way Thy way, my life Thy life,
    that all the music of my soul be but one note,
    Thyself.
O Mystery of Love, unsearchable that I the outcast
    by Thee am lifted into Life, *with* Thee in
    sweetness intercourse may suffer here, en-
    during to the end, *in* Thee be fed with daily
    Bread, Thy Life alone sufficing me.
O Love, give fear, that trembling in most holy
    dread I may receive Thy love and never keep
    my own.

For Love is Love, and naught unloving may be found in Thee.

Thy unity of Love be all my care, and not one soul in all the world be absent from my prayer, so that the world may know Thy love.

O Love, teach us to see the wounds that we have caused, the rents and tears, the schism and distress within Thy Body here on earth, so that in penitence and self-forgetfulness in Thee our prayer may be Thy prayer; that all may be restored in Thee, that through the world may be one song, one praise, one harmony with the eternal song of Love to Love in Love.

> Praise and glory ever be
> To Father, Son, and Holy Ghost,
> Three Persons ever one
> Eternal Trinity.

BIBLIOGRAPHY

THE following is a list of the books read and used in the actual preparation of this volume, or contributing in the course of my reading during the years to the conclusions expressed. Books that have been specially helpful are marked * or **.

A word might be added respecting the remarkable "Christian Library," edited and published by John Wesley. It first appeared in 1750 in fifty volumes, but my edition, of which the date is 1819, consists of thirty large octavo volumes.

Wesley, in his autocratic fashion, required his early preachers to spend not less than four hours daily in reading these volumes.

Alleine, Joseph, *Counsel for Personal Godliness.* (Wesley's Christian Library.)

Amann, Professor, *The Church of the Early Centuries.* (Sands & Co.)

**Andrewes, Bishop, *Private Prayers.* Alexander Whyte's translation. (Oliphant, Anderson and Ferrier.)

> Twenty years have passed since Dr. Alexander Whyte gave the writer a copy of his translation of Bishop Andrewes' *Private Prayers.* This was a landmark in life's journey. There is an old saying that if anyone prays with Bishop Andrewes for one week, he will wish to pray with him until the end of his life. It is impossible to overstate the value of the wonderful devotions of this English saint.

Arndt, John, *True Christianity.* (Wesley's Christian Library.)

Asceticism, The Ideals of. C. Hardman. (S.P.C.K.)

**Augustine, St., *Confessions*. Various editions.

> There is no more helpful work in the whole range of devotional literature outside of the sacred canon than the *Confessions* of St. Augustine.

—— *The Works of.* (T. & T. Clark.)

D'Avila, Don Juan (St. John of The Cross), *Spiritual Letters*. (Wesley's Christian Library.)

*—— *The Dark Night of the Soul*. (Burns & Oates.)

Baker, Fr. Augustine, *Holy Wisdom*. (Burns & Oates.)

*Baxter, Richard, *Saint's Everlasting Rest*. (Wesley's Christian Library.)

*Benedict, St., *A Character Study*. Abbot Herwegen, O.S.B. (Sands & Co.)

*Benson, Richard Meux, *Letters*. (A. R. Mowbray.)

*—— *Further Letters*. (A. R. Mowbray.)

Bernard, St., of Clairvaux, Life and Times of. James Cotter Morison. (Chapman & Hall.)

Besse, Dom, O.R.C., *The Science of Prayer*. (Burns & Oates.)

Butler, Dom Cuthbert, *Western Mysticism*. (Constable.)

Bounds, E. M., *Power through Prayer*. (Marshall, Morgan and Scott.)

Bourignon, Antoinette, *Treatise of Solid Virtue*. (Wesley's Christian Library.)

Brown, William Adams, *The Life of Prayer in a World of Science*. (Hodder & Stoughton.)

Cadman, S. Parkes, *The Plain Man's use of the Bible*. An introduction to the priceless *Bible Readers' Manual*. Edited by Charles H. Wright, D.D. (Collins, London & New York.)

> This is an invaluable handbook to the devotional studies of the Scriptures.

Carter, T. T., *Treasury of Devotion*. (Longmans.)

Cary, Lucius, *Audi Filia*. (A. R. Mowbray.)

St. Catherine of Siena. Edmund G. Gardner. (J. M. Dent.)

Chantal, St. J. F., *Selected Letters*. (Burns & Oates.)

Cisneros, Abbot Garcia de, *Book of Exercises for the Spiritual Life*.

Clements, Bernard, O.S.B., *How to Pray*. (S.P.C.K.)

Dearmer, Percy, *The Sanctuary*. (Rivingtons.)

St. Dominic, Life of. Bede Jarrett, O.P. (Burns & Oates.)

*Eudes, St. John, *The Reign of Christ*. (Burns & Oates.)

*Faber, F. W., *All for Jesus*. (Burns & Oates.)

Fenelon, Archbishop, Life of. Viscount St. Cyres. (Methuen.)

—— *Letters on the Love of God*. (Wesley's Christian Library.)

**Fosdick, H. E. *The Meaning of Prayer*. (Student Christian Movement.)

> This little handbook has a wide and well-deserved circulation on both sides of the Atlantic.

Foucauld, Charles de, Life of. René Bazin. (Burns, Oates and Washbourne.)

Fox, George, *Journal Abridged*. (Isbister.)

Francis of Assisi, Life of. Paul Sabatier. (Hodder & Stoughton.)

—— G. K. Chesterton. (Hodder & Stoughton.)

—— Father Cuthbert, O.S.F.C. (Longmans.)

—— *The Mysticism of*. W. S. Nicholson. (Jonathan Cape.)

—— Leopold de Cherance. (Burns & Oates.)

**Francis de Sales, *Introduction to the Devout Life*. (Burns & Oates.)

**—— *The Love of God*. (Burns & Oates.)

Gore, Charles, *The Philosophy of the Good Life*. (John Murray.)

Gregory, Eleanor C., *English Mystics, A Little Book of Heavenly Wisdom*. (Methuen.)

*Grou, Abbe J., *Manual for Interior Souls*. (Burns & Oates.)

Gryon, Jean Marie, *A Method of Prayer*. (J. Clarke & Co.)

Hepher, Cyril, *The Fellowship of Silence*. (Macmillan.)

Hobhouse, Stephen, *William Law and Eighteenth Century Quakerism*. (George Allen & Unwin.)

**Hügel, Baron von, *St. Catherine of Genoa, The Mystical Element of Religion as Studied in St. Catherine and her Friends, Selected Letters.* (J. M. Dent.)

*—— *Readings from.* Selected by Algar Thorold. (J. M. Dent.)

*—— *Letters to a Niece.* (J. M. Dent.)

Hughes, Hugh Price, *The Life of.* By His Daughter. (Hodder & Stoughton.)

Huvelin, Abbé, *The Love of Our Lord.* (Burns & Oates.)

Inge, W. R., *Christian Mysticism.* Bampton Lecture for 1899. (Methuen.)

Johnson, Samuel, *Prayers and Meditations.* (Allenson.)

Julian of Norwich, The Revelations of. (Burns & Oates.)

**Kirk, K. E., *The Vision of God.* Bampton Lecture for 1928. (Longmans.)
    A most valuable book. The Basis of Chapter VI.

Knox, Wilfred, *Meditation and Mental Prayer.* (Philip Allen.)

Loyola, Ignatius, *The Founder of the Jesuits.* Paul van Dyke. (Scribners.)

—— *An Attempt at an Impartial Biography.* H. H. Sedgewick. (Macmillan.)

—— *Life of.* Christopher Hollis. (Sheed & Ward.)

—— *Spiritual Exercises.* Various editions.

Maclean, Alistair B. D., *High Country.* (Inverness: Northern Counties Printing Co. Ltd.)

Maritain, J., *Prayer and Intelligence.* (Sheed & Ward.)

Oman, John, *Vision and Authority.* (Hodder & Stoughton.)

Orchard, W. E., *Prayer, its Philosophy, Practice and Power.* (Eyre & Spottiswood.)

**Pedro de Alcantara, San, *On Prayer and Meditation.* (Burns & Oates.)
    One of the most helpful Manuals.

Penn, William, *No Cross, No Crown.* (Office of the Society of Friends.)

*Plus, R., *How to Pray Always.* (Burns & Oates.)

—— *How to Pray Well.* (Burns & Oates.)

Power of Prayer, The, edited by W. P. Paterson and David Russell. (Macmillan.)

*Russell, A. J., *For Sinners Only*. (Hodder & Stoughton.)
> This is a very remarkable and vivid record of the "Oxford Groups" and their use of Meditation for *"Guidance,"* in what they term "The Quiet Hour."

Sadhu, Sundar Singh. Friedrich Heiler. (George Allen & Unwin.)

Sanders, E. K., *Sainte Chantal 1572-1641. A Study in Vocation*. (S.P.C.K.)

Scupoli, *Spiritual Combat*. (Longmans.)

*Taylor, Jeremy, *Holy Living and Dying*. (Longmans.)

*Teresa, Saint, *Her Life and Times*. Gabriela Cunninghame Graham. (Evelyn Nash.)

*—— *The Way of Perfection*. (Thomas Baker.)

*Thomas Aquinas, Saint, *On Prayer and Contemplation*. (Burns & Oates.)

**Thomas à Kempis, *The Imitation of Christ*. Various editions.

Theologica Germanica. (Macmillan.)

Underhill, Evelyn, *Mysticism*. (Methuen.)

*—— *The Mystic Way*. (J. M. Dent.)

*—— *The Mystics of the Church*. (James Clarke.)

—— Francis, *Prayer in Modern Life*. (Mowbray.)

*Vernet, Felix, *Medieval Spirituality*. (Sands & Co.)

**Wesley, John, *Works of*. Fourteen volumes. (Methodist Publishing House.)

—— *Letters of*. Edited by John Telford. 8 vols. (Methodist Publishing House.)

—— **Journal of*. Edited by Nehemiah Curnock. (Methodist Publishing House.)

—— *Life of*. Arnold Lunn. (Cassells.)

—— Charles, *A Study*. Dora M. Jones. (Skeffington.)

Wilson, Bishop, *Sacra Privata*. (Methuen.)

Workman, Herbert B., *Evolution of the Monastic Ideal*. (Methodist Publishing House.)

—— *John Wyclif, A Study of the Medieval English Church*. (Oxford University Press.)

INDEX

K

L

M

N

O

PRINTED BY W. HEFFER AND SONS LTD., CAMBRIDGE, ENGLAND.